Professions
and the State:
The Mexican Case

Highly trained professionals are increasingly important players in the power structures of Third World countries. Few studies, however, treat professional consolidation in Asia, Africa, and Latin America, and no book deals specifically with so vital a country as Mexico. This study focuses on major professions in modern Mexico: law, medicine, economics, agronomy, and petroleum engineering. The author, after a decade of Ford Foundation experience in Latin America, examines how a relatively foreign concept, professionalization, is superimposed on cultural, historical, and political patterns. The book treats conflicts affecting nationalism, university training, unemployment, prestige, self-aggrandizement, and public policy-making. The book finds that aspiring professional groups are progressively displacing lawyers at the upper echelons of political power in Mexico, and describes the changes this trend will signify for the way the state manages potentially disruptive economic and social pressures.

Professions
and the State:
The Mexican Case

PETER S. CLEAVES

The University of Arizona Press

TUCSON

THE UNIVERSITY OF ARIZONA PRESS

Copyright © 1987
The Arizona Board of Regents
All Rights Reserved

This book was set in 10/11½ VIP Baskerville.
Manufactured in the U.S.A.

Library of Congress Cataloging-in-Publication Data

Cleaves, Peter S.
Professions and the state.

(Profmex monograph series)
Bibliography: p.
Includes index.
1. Professional employees—Government policy—
Mexico.   2. Professions—Government policy—
Mexico.   3. Professional education—Mexico.
4. Economists—Mexico—Political activity.
5. Petroleum engineers—Mexico—Political activity.
6. Agriculturists—Mexico—Political activity.
7. Physicians—Mexico—Political activity.
8. Trade and professional associations—Mexico.
9. Trade-unions—Professional employees—
Mexico. I. Title.   II. Series.
HD8038.M6C55   1987   331.7'12'0972   87-5911
ISBN 0-8165-1016-4 (alk. paper)

British Library Cataloguing in Publication data are available.

With love, To
Geoffrey and Rachel

Contents

TABLES AND FIGURE

Tables

Figure

Preface

This book treats historical developments in the Mexican professions, especially their implications for politics. The analysis extends mainly to medicine, law, agronomy, petroleum engineering, and economics. The selection deliberately includes those professions that play a prominent role in the management of the state. One of the book's objectives is to assess the degree of consolidation of these professions in terms of influencing state policy. Another is to discover how the evolution of professionalism in Mexico is affected by the peculiar nature of the Mexican political system. A third objective is to provide the general reader with clues to the issues facing professions in Mexico: ideological cleavages, member associations, career advancement, and international versus national university training. The reader will soon discover that professional development in Mexico cannot be judged by those standards prevalent in liberal capitalist systems that have generated most prevailing notions of professional autonomy, responsibility, and prerogatives.

The book takes a tentatively "pro-profession" perspective, conditional upon the values Mexican professions espouse during consolidation. The bias is predicated on a presumption that, under effective leadership, professional development (likely to evolve mainly within the state) can represent a net benefit to Mexican society. Should leadership stress particularistic rather than universalistic objectives for the professions and ignore ethical issues, the result will not necessarily be a qualitative change in the management of the Mexican state.

The book will be successful if it sparks additional interest in a fascinating subject. My involvement stems from a decade of collaboration with Latin Americans in building professional cadres in the region. While with the Ford Foundation, I recognized early on that professionalism is evolving differently in Latin America than in the United States and Britain. Concerned that no existing model of professional development is appropriate to explain the emerging patterns, and that relatively simplistic assumptions guide most beliefs about the implications of professional training, I determined to address the question of professional development as a sociological and political theme. Professionals represent a privileged subgroup of Third World societies, and their intervention in the political and bureaucratic sphere is increasingly important for policy formation and implementation. The theme of professionalism has hardly been examined by scholars of change in the Third World, and reliable quantitative data are notoriously absent. The thinness of this volume should alert the reader that the chapters that follow do not pretend to be definitive. The intent is to begin to fill a void in the literature, while stimulating studies in greater depth into professions in Mexico and elsewhere.

A portion of the information for this book was gathered during one or more private interviews with members of the five professions mentioned above. The sample, totaling forty-three persons, was not scientifically selected, as evidenced by the fact that all were interviewed in Mexico City. Nevertheless, many of these persons had held leadership posts and were highly respected in their professional ranks (see Appendix). All occupy or have occupied a public sector or university position, and all were candid in speaking of the challenges facing their professions, partially because they were promised that their comments would be treated anonymously. The comparative literature on professions contributed another set of insights to this study. Detailed analyses of professions in Latin America and the Third World are regrettably few. The majority of existing research deals with British and U.S. examples. The small body of writing on professional and technical roles in relatively centralized systems, such as those in Continental and Eastern Europe, proved to be helpful in understanding the Mexican case. This examination may be suggestive of broad themes in professional development elsewhere and may point to methods of analyzing a diverse set of country-specific cases.

I owe a debt of gratitude to a number of individuals and institutions who assisted me in the preparation of this book. The interviewees contributed generously of their time and interpretations, and permitted me to quote liberally from their remarks. Several Mexican professionals and fellow social scientists read the manuscript, helped correct errors, and thus improved the final version. Special thanks are extended to Pablo Latapí, Emilio Alanís, Viviane Márquez, Roderic Camp, Eliot Freidson, Larissa Lomnitz, and David Greenwood. In my mind, this book will always be associated with the late Rainer Godau, who provided inspiration in the early writing stages, and whose tragic departure left his family, friends, and colleagues with an irreparable loss. My employer in Mexico, the Ford Foundation, provided logistical support while I researched and wrote the first version of the manuscript, as did The First National Bank of Chicago in the later stages. The Northwestern University Library was a valuable depository of secondary sources. Araceli Marín and Luz María Montaño patiently typed interview notes and several drafts, and were helpful in tracking down bibliographical references. My wife Dorothy and my children were (on the whole) supportive of my taking time from family life to concentrate on the project, and so I dedicate the book with love and gratitude to Geoffrey and Rachel.

None of these individuals or institutions, however, bears any blame for inadvertent lapses in fact or judgment that may impair this book. The final responsibility lies fully with the author himself.

P.S.C.
Chicago, Illinois

List of Acronyms

AMEAS	Mexican Association of Higher Agricultural Studies	(Asociación Mexicana de Educación Agrícola Superior)
ANUIES	National Association of Universities and Institutes of Higher Education	(Asociación Nacional de Universidades e Institutos de Educación Superior)
BANOBRAS	National Bank of Public Works and Services	(Banco Nacional de Obras y Servicios Públicos)
BANRURAL	National Rural Credit Bank	(Banco Nacional de Crédito Rural)
CANACINTRA	National Chamber for Manufacturing Industries	(Cámara Nacional de la Industria de la Transformación)
CEPAL	Economic Commission for Latin America, United Nations (ECLA)	(Comisión Económica para la América Latina)
CFE	Federal Electricity Commission	(Comisión Federal de Electricidad)
CIMMYT	International Maize and Wheat Improvement Center	(Centro Internacional de Mejoramiento de Maíz y Trigo)

CNC	National Peasants Confederation	(Confederación Nacional Campesina)
CONCAMIN	Confederation of Chambers of Industries	(Confederación de Cámaras Industriales)
CONCANACO	Confederation of National Chambers of Commerce	(Confederación de Cámaras Nacionales de Comercio)
CONACYT	Science and Technology Council	(Consejo Nacional de Ciencia y Tecnología)
CONASUPO	National Enterprise for Basic Food Products	(Compañía Nacional de Subsistencias Populares)
CTM	Mexican Workers Confederation	(Confederación de Trabajadores de México)
DIF	Institute for Integrated Family Development	(Desarrollo Integral de la Familia)
ENA	National School of Agriculture	(Escuela Nacional de Agricultura)
ENE	National School of Economics	(Escuela Nacional de Economía)
GATT	General Agreement on Tariffs and Trade	
ILPES	Latin American Institute for Economic and Social Planning	(Instituto Latino-americano de Planificación Económica y Social)
IMCE	Mexican Foreign Commerce Institute	(Instituto Mexicano de Comercio Exterior)
IMF	International Monetary Fund	
IMP	Mexican Petroleum Institute	(Instituto Mexicano del Petróleo)
IMSS	Mexican Social Security Institute	(Instituto Mexicano del Seguro Social)
INIA	National Institute for Agricultural Research	(Instituto Nacional de Investigación Agrícola)
IPN	National Polytechnical Institute	(Instituto Politécnico Nacional)

ISSSTE	Social Security and Services Institute for Public Employees	(Instituto de Seguridad y Servicios Sociales para los Trabajadores del Estado)
ITAM	Autonomous Technological Institute of Mexico	(Instituto Tecnológico Autónomo de México)
ITESM	Monterrey Institute of Technology	(Instituto Tecnológico de Estudios Superiores de Monterrey)
NAFINSA	National Development Bank	(Nacional Financiera S.A.)
OECD	Organization for Economic Cooperation and Development	
PEMEX	Mexican Petroleum Company	(Petróleos Mexicanos)
PNUD	United Nations Development Program	(Programa de las Naciones Unidas para el Desarrollo)
PRI	Revolutionary Institutional Party	(Partido Revolucionario Institucional)
SAHOP	Secretariat of Human Settlements and Public Works	(Secretaría de Asentamientos Humanos y Obras Públicas)
SAM	Mexican Food System	(Sistema Alimentario Mexicano)
SARH	Secretariat of Agriculture and Hydraulic Resources	(Secretaría de Agricultura y Recursos Hidráulicos)
SDN	Secretariat of National Defense	(Secretaría de la Defensa Nacional)
SEPAFIN	Secretariat of National Properties and Industries	(Secretaría de Patrimonio y Fomento Industrial)
SSA	Secretariat of Health and Welfare	(Secretaría de Salubridad y Asistencia)
UDUAL	Latin American University Union	(Unión de Universidades de América Latina)

| UNAM | National Autonomous University of Mexico, also called the National University | (Universidad Nacional Autónoma de México, o Universidad Nacional) |
| UNESCO | United Nations Educational, Scientific, and Cultural Organization | |

CHAPTER 1

Mexican Professions Compared

Economic development has led to extensive division of labor in Mexico. Consequently, professional specialties within the occupational structure have proliferated and new kinds of professionals have emerged in top policy-making positions. Whereas only twenty-three professions were officially recognized in the 1944 Law of Professions, the number increased to sixty-six in the 1973 reform of that law, with provisions for further additions on a relatively open-ended basis. The title *profesionista* refers to a multitude of positions that in the recent past were held by *técnicos, maestros,* or did not exist at all. Students flock to enroll in the universities' professional programs and graduate in record numbers. Employers complain about the poor technical and academic preparation of graduates, who exceed by a large margin the number of available jobs. Despite the erosion of quality, outstanding individuals still emerge in the traditional fields of law, medicine, and engineering to assume positions of national leadership.

Since the 1940s lawyers have predominated in the political sphere, holding most top positions in the cabinet and the PRI, the official Revolutionary Institutional Party. From Miguel Alemán to Miguel de la Madrid, six of seven presidents of the country have been lawyers. Recently, individuals with other types of professional training have infringed on the lawyers' monopoly in sectors pertaining to their specialized fields. Under the López Portillo presidency, for instance, economists almost completely displaced lawyers in the nation's financial and monetary institutions, and agronomists, social scientists, and basic scientists were promoted promoted to higher positions than previously was the case in governmental agencies that corresponded to their specialties.

Some analysts might consider this trend to be a subtle one compared with other major political issues confronting the Mexican nation, such as petroleum development, external debt, urbanization, food production, employment, redistribution, and foreign relations. This study argues that professional development and the further consolidation of the Mexican state are mutually interrelated. The assertion has implications for how and where professionals exercise power, and for the burden of responsibility they bear for the way that power is used. Most Mexican professions, while implicitly engaged in strategies to increase their collective influence, are at a stage of preconsciousness. Coprofessionals who would fuse as private sector interest groups, based on expertise and adopting a critical stance vis-à-vis the state, are not likely to prevail, despite the intuitive attractiveness of the notion of professional autonomy. Those who aim to capture parts of the state, carving out an exclusive sphere of influence, are more likely to succeed, but they must assume normative responsibility for the state's behavior, especially in the sectors under their control. The line between statism and professionalism in Mexico promises to become increasingly blurred from now to the end of the century.

HISTORICAL CONTRASTS

Mexican economic development has rested essentially on private capitalism, with a helping hand from the state in providing financial support and political control of labor.[1] The development of the Mexican professions, however, has not proceeded in the same way as in other capitalist societies, such as the United States and Great Britain. Most of the literature available in the field of sociology of the professions has been based on British and U.S. cases.[2] These writings suggest useful themes for study but are unfaithful predictors of the behavior of Mexican professions.[3]

The reasons are many. First, the consolidation of the Mexican state preceded the growth of professions. In medieval England, the professions originated in the guilds and corporations, which, although officially recognized by the state, exercised considerable autonomy in maintaining technical standards and governing employment. The Inns of Court flourished in the fifteenth century, and London's Royal College of Physicians was licensing doctors in the sixteenth century, meaning that lawyers and medical doctors had functioning professional associations in Britain well before Cromwell's centralizing reforms.[4] Although the level of activity in these associations varied, and occasionally they were moribund, the early date of their incorporation had clear consequences. As the state grew in importance, the professional groups held sway over legal dictates governing their fields and often retained the right to certify individuals for professional practice. The United States followed the British lead, and U.S. professional associations often have had more influence over national policy than have the respective federal departments.

In the Iberian peninsula and, by extension, in Hispanic America, the legacy of guilds did not evolve into independent industrial, educational, or commercial entities, but into corporate structures with greater scope than in the middle ages. Delays in capitalist development extended the vitality of such vertical institutions as the church, the military, the monarchy, and the traditional professions. These functional hierarchies remained ethically and politically beholden to the crown, and later to the national state. In early twentieth-century Mexico the tumultuous 1910 Revolution disrupted and displaced the traditional professions, which during the Porfiriato resembled their Iberic brethren. The subsequent consolidation of the modern state preempted any move by new groups of doctors and engineers to establish independent lodges. Rather, they merged with the state as the state grew, lending their skills to a consensual model of national development, but not contributing a unique definition to that model. Later, when the number of professionals grew in the post-war period, the task of articulating profession-based criteria on the state's role was more difficult because the state was already entrenched.

Second, the state apparatus is the most important employer of Mexican professionals, including those in the fields of law, medicine, agronomy, and several branches of engineering.[5] Professionals in Britain and the United States are not all private practitioners. Depending on the field, they work as individuals, in consulting teams, or for institutions. The dominant groups, however, are in the private sector and/or work under professionals in management positions. Debate within the professions revolves around barriers to university entrance, client relations, fee schedules, and lobbying. Satisfactory professional-client relations are a resource professionals use to multiply their political influence. Professionals barter their legitimate expertise in one sphere for broader influence in public policy, and they are most successful when their reputation is relatively unsullied and society is dependent on their services. Spread about geographically and interacting with a relatively atomized public, these professionals engage in self-regulation to maintain their status and income and to mobilize collective power to preserve a favorable climate for their operations.

When professionals work primarily for organizations and those agencies are within the state apparatus, as in Mexico, the configuration of inducements is different. Professionals work for managers, rather than hiring managers to sort out their administrative affairs. Bureaucratic concerns come to the fore, such as their relations with line supervisors, who tend to be unsympathetic to professional work habits or standards of excellence.[6] Sometimes professionals join unions to try to protect their interests within the bureaucracy. The principal reference group is not the individual client, who neither pays for services nor can assist with career advancement. Clients are relatively useless allies in protecting the professional because, as petitioners, they frequently receive shabby treatment in the bureaucracy. Consequently, professionals strike alliances with power-holders within the organization. Since the employer is the state, they seek support from complementary entities such as high-level administrators, politicians, and legislators. Under such circumstances, the bargaining power of professionals declines and their professional independence is subjected to multiple compromises.

Third, Mexican professionals usually are not authors of their own technology. In advanced industrialized countries, ample university and government research, combined with efficient information systems, permit the professions to innovate techniques and to create wholly new technological approaches in their fields. In olden times, leading clergymen, architects, and engineers in Europe, the world center of the epoch, radiated their learning throughout their own societies and to the periphery.[7] In the modern era, medical and agricultural scientists have achieved remarkable advances in the United States and Western Europe, and have seen their techniques permeate worldwide professional networks. The esteem earned by world-class professionals helps legitimate the autonomy of the professions within their own national boundaries, even in highly centralized systems. Infringements on professional prerogatives are less frequent when the derivative academic community can rightly claim a string of Nobel prizes or important theoretical breakthroughs. Under such circumstances, nationalists appreciate the value of professionals and are less likely to disparage their aspirations for autonomy.

In Mexico, the situation is quite reversed. Except for the field of law, which is a priori nation-bound, the professions are highly dependent on knowledge generated abroad. This dependence, of course, is not uniform, and a few Mexican professionals have made important contributions to international thinking in their fields. Nonetheless, the economic reality is that most research and development in medicine, engineering, agronomy, and economics is accomplished in the richer countries, which can afford such luxuries. Internationalist professionals in Mexico are so oriented because they feel an obligation to stay up-to-date with new developments and to apply them in their own work. Sub-groups often emerge that strive to reconcile their professional orientation with the unique needs of the nation. Although their approaches often are technically inferior, they may achieve equal or greater recognition than colleagues whose training and technical rigor are in the mainstream of the profession worldwide. Some nationalists belittle the work of their internationalist colleagues as being foreign-inspired, aggravating a tension between professionalism and nationalism. The division between both kinds of professionals can be acrimonious, and their disputes can impair the profession's reputation in society.

Fourth, Mexican professions have multiple and competing professional associations. The major professions in Britain and the United States have created associations that tend toward monopolization of representative functions. Among these are the Institute of Civil Engineers (founded in 1818), the British Medical Association (1832), the American Dental Association (1840), and the American Medical Association (1847).[8] The historical circumstances surrounding the founding of these various bodies has been different. Often they represented an attempt to unify lesser groups or societies that employed widely different criteria for certifying entrance into the profession. While an act of national legislation often assisted the organizational effort, the associations were not dependent on the state. Even in their incipient forms, the professional bodies were the sponsors of these laws, which established momentum for subsequent lobbying efforts. The associations provide important services to their members, including journals, conferences, mechanisms for conflict resolution, diffusion of new techniques, and, in most cases, either directly or indirectly, licensing. It is important that while a professional might join a more specialized or subsidiary association, his affiliation with the primary institution in the field tends to remain active; infrequently do two or more professional associations of national scope compete for the allegiance of the same members.

While many Mexican associations have had outstanding leadership, they serve different functions than do their counterparts in Europe and the United States. In the first place, they can offer very little to their membership to inspire allegiance or create dependence. According to the Law of Professions, their purview is limited to peripheral matters, such as collaborating with universities to draw up course curricula, organizing professional conferences, and proposing fee schedules.[9] They are not endowed with authority to maintain standards of competency or certify professional skills. Many associations become arenas for ambitious bureaucrats (who incidently hold a professional degree) to gain honorary posts, in the expectation of distinguishing themselves for high appointments in the state bureaucracy. New associations spring up with the change of Mexican presidencies, so that a greater number of aspirants can claim that they lead a national profession in their field. The manipulation of these posts dampens the enthusiasm of other professionals to participate in association affairs.

Fifth, the Mexican professions have no formal mechanisms to bar entrance, certify competence, or expel the unqualified. General examinations are common in the United States and Europe, where lawyers, doctors, engineers, dentists, and druggists are required to pass regional or national boards to practice their professions legally. These tests are administered either by the respective professional association or the state. When offered by the state, the professional associations usually are prominently represented on the examination boards. The examinations tend to be more exacting than the requirements to graduate from the leading universities in the field, and many students fail them on more than one occasion. In cases of professional incompetence or moral turpitude, elaborate mechanisms exist to withdraw the license to practice. In some specialties, professionals are required to take periodic examinations to assure that they have not allowed their knowledge to lapse.

In Mexico, a university degree is sufficient for certifying that an individual is competent to practice a profession. Once an academic program in the private or state university system is authorized, its graduates qualify for the professional license (*cédula*), which is automatically extended by the General Agency of Professions in the Secretariat of Public Education. (Naturally, additional approvals often are necessary actually to practice the profession, such as a building permit for civil engineers.) The criteria for authorizing professional programs in the universities are not strict. Consequently, at least forty-six programs exist in medicine, forty-two in law, fifty-eight in engineering, and thirty-eight in agronomy, many of them suffering from poor libraries and laboratories, few full-time faculty, and lax quality standards.

Open admissions policies in state universities have led to "massification" of the student body and to a severe overproduction of many types of professionals beyond the market's ability to absorb them. The General Agency of Professions has not recorded cases of a professional license being revoked for demonstrated incompetence. In short, restrictions on entry to the university, on graduation, and on professional practice are loose. Most controls are economic in nature: whether the students' families can afford to subsidize their children during their university program, and whether the national economy can produce additional jobs for the multitude of professionals seeking employment.

Sixth, professional prestige is less stable in Mexico than in societies where professions were consolidated before the twentieth century and where access today is limited. In the United States and Britain, professional leaders before the Industrial Revolution came from the modernizing wings of the aristocracy, which lent status to their occupations. Traditional professions warded off periodic attempts to undermine their legitimacy. Prestige rankings are remarkably constant, irrespective of social class, geographic location, and historical moment.[10]

In Mexico, major traditional professions dating from the Colonial period are the clergy, military, law and medicine. Two of these have suffered declines in the twentieth century. State doctrine denigrates priests and discriminates against the military. The professional prestige of these fields (plus law, implicated in corruption) is ambiguous. While *profesionista* conjures up a positive image for lower-class groups aspiring for mobility, these groups appear to be as mystified by the subtle status differences between economists and engineers as are elites concerning that between cobblers and janitors.[11] The prestige of professions in Mexico appears to fluctuate from region to region, over time (depending on whether, for instance, government priorities are public works or financial affairs), and among individuals whose total impression of the profession is based on personal contact with a single practitioner. Easy access to professional degrees and high unemployment in some fields further confound status variables. The sample of professional elites interviewed for this study ranked medicine as the most prestigious of six fields, followed by engineering, law, architecture, economics, and agronomy.[12] However, these professionals often disagreed on the criteria for professional prestige and deference due subfields in their own disciplines.[13] Critical remarks about colleagues' competence disrupts professional unity and attenuates professionals' claim to societal respect.

THEORETICAL ISSUES

It follows that general hypotheses concerning the development of professions in England and the United States are not always appropriate for Mexico. The literature in general argues that the greater the organizational consolidation of the professional group, and the greater the dependence of the society on its skills, the more opportunities there are for professionals to rise in political influence, social status, and material gain.[14] These propositions may have the false attribute of "universal validity." Although self-evident, they cannot claim to be "universally relevant" because strong professional associations, membership barriers, common norms, and minimal guarantees for autonomy are absent in many societies, Mexico included.

Can Mexico claim to have professions if these attributes of professional life are absent? This question is far from trivial. The sociological literature of the 1950s and 1960s is replete with descriptions of the functional characteristics of professions. In these writings, a profession is an occupation involving specialized knowledge, high-level educational training, control over the content of work, self-organization and self-regulation, altruism and community service, and high ethical standards. Such writers as Parsons, Barber, and Wilensky intuitively sensed that "professions" were a special form of occupational organization.[15] Their descriptive phrases, however, were not quantifiable or especially helpful in distinguishing between professions and normal occupations. After surveying the field, one skeptic was prompted to call these attributes a "strange mixture of propositions of the most varied nature including, as if they were compatible, empirical generalizations, a priori definitions, conditional relationships which, by means of semantic ambiguities, are dressed up as empirical fact."[16].

Another school, made up of critical theorists, views professions in terms of social stratification: i.e., another form of inequality such as class, race, or sex. Prominent writers in this vein are Larson, Illich, Johnson, Frankenberg, Boreham, Pemberton, and Wilson.[17] They claim that practitioners of certain occupations, to enhance their earnings and prestige, strive to create a monopoly over the performance of tasks valued by the society at large. Such professional attributes as association, ethics, and altruism "can often be best understood as *strategies* for the achievement and maintenance of a particular type of occupational control . . . which grants power and prestige to the practitioners."[18] The implication is that professions do not have intrinsic characteristics but evolve from the deliberately self-serving motives of the profession's founders.

While the functional school may be too elementary, the critical school seems voluntaristic. All modern societies have (and apparently need) professions, but their form, content, and status differ for cultural, historical, and institutional reasons. For the purposes of this study, a profession is a *privileged occupation with mystique.* Profession, as such, is not a distinct sociological category. The concept depends on arbitrary measures of occupational coherence (e.g., technical unity), privilege (nonmanual labor, high income), and mystique (including charisma and prestige, and what has been called "indeterminacy").[19] A limitation of the functional and critical approaches to the study of professions is that both are tied to liberal capitalist societies. The former school espouses a benign interpretation of professions as part of a defense of liberalism. The latter turns professional ethics and public service on their head as part of a rejection of capitalism. These writings have limited applicability to societies where liberalism is absent or capitalism weak.

Randall Collins has advanced the state of the art in his cross-national and historical analysis of professional occupations.[20] His work merges concepts of political power, technology, and "culture." Culture refers both to the self-conscious mores of the professional group, and to the norms and expectations of the society at large. Collins' theory of professions is "a theory of group formation, status, strength of boundaries, relationship of domination and subordination, and various degrees of property in the form of occupational 'positions'." The degree of centralization and decentralization of states "plays a large part in the volatility of cultural markets, thus having an indirect effect upon the formation of occupational communities, as well as a direct effect through state intervention in legally shaping positional property."[21] Interestingly, Collins does not stress expertise as a predominant source of professional power. Collins's own examples, and the independent work of other scholars, help substantiate the approach, which is useful for differentiating Britain and the United States from nineteenth-century Germany and France and from contemporary socialist societies, which have had centralist government systems. They also suggest relevant features of professions in many developing countries.

As in Mexico, the emergence of professions in "underdeveloped" Prussia was not isolated from the growth of the state. The Prussian *Generaldirektorium* was consolidated in the eighteenth century when Prussia was a backwater of Europe. The civil service was made up of Junkers, aristocrats, and bourgeois who were obedient to the state and whose social origins endowed them with status.[22] The "bureaucrat's training gave him the aura of an expert; in German society, expertise gave one the right to act authoritatively . . . . Everyone else should defer to him—and in fact often did."[23] Rueschemeyer points out that the nineteenth-century lawyer's juridical discretion was limited by the weight of German civil codes, and discretion was minimal.[24] He would agree with LaVopa that "professionalization" is an Anglo-Saxon concept which, when transplanted to Central Europe, has limited analytical utility. In studying Prussian school teachers, LaVopa prefers the concept of "professional emancipation," which meant occupying a position between society and state and enjoying the best of both worlds. Professional independence meant "both official power vis-à-vis the public and a degree of corporate autonomy in the official ranks. The . . . pursuit of both goals may have been integral to the professional ethos in nineteenth-century Germany."[25]

Prior to the French Revolution, the monarchy accorded privilege and position to skilled occupations that served state purposes. Engineers gained stature during the seventeenth century as builders of royal roads; after the Revolution, Napoleon helped them perpetuate their position by founding the Ecole Polytechnique, the first of the *grades écoles*.[26] In French medicine, the ethos of public service emerged in the seventeenth century as doctors were called upon to combat epidemics and plagues.[27] In the nineteenth century, the public health *medecin* working for the state still enjoyed higher prestige than did the private practitioner, who was often considered a quack.[28] While English lawyers sought private clients, French lawyers studied codified law in the national universities and looked for professional careers in the public administration. Professional prestige in both France and Germany was coterminus with public sector employment.

In contemporary socialist systems, prestige rankings for professional fields and ideas of professional autonomy contrast with those in liberal capitalist systems. Engineering, for example, is more highly regarded in the Soviet Union (and France) than in Britain (or the United States). Within the Soviet Union, physicists outrank engineers, and medical researchers outrank doctors.[29] In his study of Cuban medicine, Richard Garfield notes that it is "more appropriate to judge the socialist type of professionalism . . . by its *interactive* than *autonomous* character. Those professions, which once enjoyed independence, such as medicine, have lost it."[30] Professionalism is characterized by teamwork, by egalitarian esprit de corps, by evaluation of superiors by subordinates, and by tight regulation by state ministries. Garfield thus takes exception to those who think, as a general rule, of "government intervention, the reduction of autonomy, and the elimination of private employment as forces which lower quality."[31] Rather, the designation of "professions" in centralist systems involves different occupations, privileges, and prestige than in liberal capitalist systems.

The functional theorists (especially Parsons, Merton, and Barber) identify professions as special occupations. The critical theorists (such as Larson) perceive their emergence in class terms. Collins observes that professions differ in important respects depending on whether the political system tends toward liberalism or centralism. He does not provide many theoretical leads for intermediate, hybrid, or corporatist systems, such as those often found in Latin America. Thus his work, too, is not fully applicable to the Mexican case.

THE POLITICAL CONTEXT

The role of professionals in the state depends on the kind of state in which they are immersed and the state's need for their services. Different kinds of states foster different levels of professional authority, organization, and initiative. The Mexican state is facing increasing technical challenges in designing and implementing public policy, and requires politicians with diverse skills and constituencies, circumstances which combine to open avenues for the exercise of professional power.

Scholars of Latin America have applied several labels to political systems in the region. These systems usually are distinguished by the degree of concentration of power in specific social classes, the role of the state in the economy, the ways in which the state builds links with organized economic interests and the popular sectors, and the ideological symbols propagated by governing elites and internalized by different elements of the population.[32] Liberal systems based on some form of electoral democracy, checks and balances, deconcentration of power, and individual rights are reemerging in Latin America from that nadir when military governments dominated the region. Even during the apogee of democratic institutions during the 1960s and early 1970s, some analysts questioned the depth of their implantation; these skeptics felt themselves vindicated by the arrival of generals in the seats of power. Nonetheless, the "rules of the game" were sufficiently well defined and accepted by the political actors for the system to resemble that of advanced industrial countries, which also shared a liberal ideology. Professions tend to behave in these systems as in Britain and the United States, where the balance of professional power is in the private sector. Professionals seek autonomy over their clients, attempt to regulate the marketplace, and pursue their class objectives as an interest group. Prestige rankings correlate with income-earning power.

A purely centralist mode also is uncommon in Latin America. Centralism is attenuated by the cultural diversity and political fragmentation of most Latin American countries, the relatively recent ascendancy of the state in the economy, and the absence of a homegrown Latin American centralist ideology.[33] Some regimes have experimented with vertical command, state control of the economy, the expulsion of dissident elements, and a synthetic ideology encompassing all segments of the nation. Except for the Cuban case, these efforts have been short-lived and have evolved into other forms. When centralism predominates, professionals find employment mainly in the state bureaucracy and their associational forms are controlled by government. Professional autonomy is achieved when persons with similar professional training succeed in penetrating all hierarchical levels of a bureaucratic sector or agency and are able to interpret and implement state ideology in a way consistent with professional interests. Prestige accrues from the privileges the state accords the professions because of their contribution to the state's objectives.

Finally, the corporatist model has been used to describe some political systems in Latin America.[34] Corporatism is most obvious when political leadership attempts to restructure society by sector as a means of undermining lower-class unity and facilitating state intervention in the economy. Such was the Peruvian case from 1969 to 1975 under the government General Juan Velasco Alvarado. Other corporatist systems evolve from a patrimonial state, such as during the Getulio Vargas period in Brazil. Under stable corporatist systems, policy-making tends to be centralized in the presidency, with little formal planning at the national level and little emphasis given to policy integration except in times of crisis. Sectoral activities concentrate on regulation and enforcement of procedures. Professional associations interpenetrate state and society, and their role is to support national integrative ideology. Their level of prestige depends on their contribution to national harmony, conflict resolution, and social peace. Under certain circumstances, the clergy and military, often considered superannuated professional groups, can rank high in prestige, as in Franco's Spain.

Mexican society has been variously defined as developing, authoritarian, tutelary, and corporatist.[35] Pablo González Casanova refers to it as a system of monopolistic liberalism.[36] The term suggests the existence of formal groups interacting and competing within a marketplace controlled by a dominant actor, namely the state and its appendages. The limits on the freedom of these groups are well understood, and the dominant actor relies mainly on market mechanisms, with occasional forceful tactics, to maintain its preeminence. The description is apt, and helps explain why Mexico and its professions are difficult to pigeonhole into one of the other categories described above.

Four overarching features of the Mexican state affect the political roles of professionals within it.

First, the Mexican state is a powerful apparatus, able to maintain effective economic, public security, and ideological controls. As the dominant force in Mexican society, the state was consolidated in the post-revolutionary period before the development of modern professions.[37] The size and power of the Mexican state represent both constraints and opportunities for Mexican professions. It is illusory for professionals to think of challenging state power in direct confrontation. Officialdom has access to sanctions and penalties sufficient to overwhelm uncountenanced behavior by individual professionals or professional groups. The state dictates the role of professionals in civil society, rather than responding to initiatives based on professional criteria. On the other hand, working within the state sector, professionals have the opportunity to harness these resources for specific ends, and to participate in the way decisions are implemented. Their technical advice often is useful for the definition of projects, plans, and approaches to national development.

Second, industrial, financial, and commercial interests are better organized and, as collectivities, have more access to the levers of political power than do other groups, such as workers, peasants, and liberal professions in civil society. The collaborative political framework has been patiently constructed since the 1940s, and has been interrupted only briefly (mainly at the rhetorical level) during the López Mateos and Echeverría years. Neither the state nor these economic actors have shown much enthusiasm for a rapid expansion of the number of participants in major decisions. The ultimate loyalty and predictability of the current participants have been proven over time, and they have learned to seek accommodations. The desired role for professional groups in this ambience is not to manifest policies that counter those previously agreed upon by the major actors, and certainly not to promote themselves as power contenders on a permanent basis. However, to the degree that they can carve out niches in the state apparatus, the system will protect them from untoward competition from other groups that are being excluded. The same insularity that reduces professionals' influence as actors in civil society improves their relative power when they control occupational space within the bureaucracy.

Third, important decision-making centers in the system are limited in number, centralized, and difficult to penetrate. Specialized interest groups face obstacles in gaining a hearing, except when their positions might relieve a serious tension in the system. Private sector professionals or those in academia who would bring the expertise of their field to bear on a major development problem have to adopt a long-term view, focus their attention on the President's Office, and wait for their dire predictions to begin to materialize before official action is proclaimed. The road to success is long and the payoff uncertain. Professionals, however, have other ways to improve their influence, despite the few locations at which policies actually are made. In sectoral ministries occupying intermediate positions, they can affect policies incrementally by controlling their implementation.[38] While the scope of their authority is narrow, their cumulative impact over time can be significant. Political leaders who might ignore some groups' class interests in adopting policies are increasingly unlikely to dismiss professional input, especially when the policy challenge is complex. Professionals can temper their behavior to earn progressive promotions to the level of agency directors or state secretaries. In the past, success often has meant they were rewarded with high-ranking posts, the responsibilities of which bore no resemblance to their previous professional training. Professionalism became diluted as their political responsibilities increased.[39] If they wished to be a candidate for the presidency, they placed a high premium on avoiding controversy, which might be unleashed by an innovative policy proposal. In the future, if professionals with similar training occupy all hierarchical positions in sector ministries, the political and professional gap is likely to narrow. The strength of the unit in bureaucratic politics will be based in part on its professional competence.

Fourth, Mexican nationalism and the symbol of the Mexican Revolution provide the means for mystifying the polity. The complex interaction between symbols and reality represents other constraints and opportunities. On the one hand, it diminishes the value of the special expertise often claimed by professionals. The purpose of "old" policies can easily be disguised, and their outcomes either obscured through restrictions on information or by identifying them with the goals of the Revolution. Policy advocates have difficulty gaining adherents for initiatives potentially beneficial to the nation as a whole when the general impression is that the existing policy is already protecting its welfare. When a position is too clearly defined or forcibly argued, its sponsors may be accused of importing "foreign ideas" that violate the essence of Mexican nationhood. These practices discourage professionals from seeking legitimacy for their views on the basis of their contribution to a rational dialogue on alternatives for national programs.

On the other hand, state-oriented professionals can couch new recommendations in terms consistent with prevailing symbols. Knowing that the full implications of a policy recommendation would generate overt opposition, professionals can subtly merge the mystique of their profession with national mythology to cloud the changes being advocated. Claiming that the policy reflects both advanced professional thinking and revolutionary precepts shifts the locus of debate to terrain they control, and heightens "indeterminacy." The mystification principle can be a nemesis or an ally, depending on their skill in using professional criteria to interpret state ideology.

Within a system of monopolistic liberalism, where control of the state apparatus is the key to social domination, those professions that contribute to that domination while catering to unifying symbols (such as nationalism and economic development) will rise in status and material reward almost irrespective of their degree of professional consolidation in civil society. This proposition does not mean that professional training and membership associations are totally inconsequential. Rather, the idea is that other factors in Mexico play a greater role in the development of the professions than does their ability to constitute themselves as authentic interest groups. The particular organization, behavioral patterns, and mores of the Mexican system affect the development of the professions, just as those of the British, French, and Soviet systems affect professions in those countries. The differences are sufficiently large, however, to alert the analyst to pervasive influences, such as nationalism, state domination, co-optation, and small group allegiance that combine in ways unique to Mexico. It is more useful to differentiate medicine, law, agronomy, petroleum engineering, and economics in Mexico along these lines than by their degree of conventional professional autonomy.[40]

Obviously, the nationalistic dimension is important in a nationalistic society, and the evolution of some professions in Mexico has been eminently more nationalistic than others. These professions have been more successful in resisting or mitigating foreign influences, especially of a technical kind. Law, for instance, is deeply rooted in the historical past. The Mexican Constitution is a unique document laden with nationalist sentiment. The legitimacy of contemporary law rests in part on popular affection for the Constitution. Over the years legal codes have adjusted to social changes inside Mexico and have borrowed little from other countries.[41] At the other extreme, medical treatment in Mexico has become almost indistinguishable from that in the United States, although the coverage is much less thorough and it is administered mainly in public sector institutes. Mexican doctors tend to be professionally intolerant of indigenous curing techniques. Although petroleum engineering is a highly technical field, it can be considered more nationalistic than many other Mexican professions because it was founded during an emotionally charged sovereign act, the expropriation of foreign oil companies. Over the years it has successfully devised procedures to maintain its national character, even though much of its technology is imported.

Professional specialties have flourished in Mexico because the state requires new and refined skills. In recent years, principal themes in the polity have been economic development and social control. While lawyers still are omnipresent in the bureaucracy, economics has risen rapidly in official favor, and properly credentialed economists have commanded superior salaries and been appointed to high posts. Despite rhetorical claims, national health and rural poverty have not been priority themes for the political system. [42] That is, leaders have not believed that reducing morbidity or increasing agricultural production is critical for maintaining social peace or raising the GNP. Consequently, the state is less dependent on doctors or agronomists, and those professionals in these fields who work in the public sector suffer in terms of remuneration and political clout.

The other side of the coin is the degree of dependence of a given profession on the state for employment.[43] Given the number of licensed professionals in Mexico, and the diversity of the political system, this calculation can be made in various ways. In a particular profession, virtually all members can be gainfully employed and work only for the state, as, for example, petroleum engineers and agronomists. Alternatively, some professionals can work only for the state, while an inadequately trained majority have no job at all related to their field, as, for example, economists. Or, the professionals are split more or less evenly between the state and private sectors, yet relatively few engage in activities strictly pertaining to their fields, as in the law profession. Finally, most members of the profession can be unemployed in their field, while the majority of those who are engaged both work for the state and have private practices, as among doctors. A greater reliance on the state for employment naturally narrows the access of individual professionals to jobs when there is a surfeit of qualified persons from which the state can choose. The scale of relative job dependence would appear to proceed from petroleum engineering (most dependent), to agronomy, economics, law, and medicine.

The weakness of professional associations does not mean that Mexican professionals act alone in seeking advancement in the system. They often rely for mutual protection on small groups or networks, in which allegiance is based on friendship, school affiliation, political orientation, or business partnerships (including letting public sector bids to companies owned by state officials). Often these ties extend beyond the profession's boundaries, especially in the less technical fields, such as law and economics. Public sector lawyers are continuously tracking the ups and downs of mutual assistance groups in the political sphere, and are by far the most sensitive "political animals" in the Mexican system. Agronomists recognize *compadrazgo* (buddy) networks, often derived from school membership, whose leaders are looked upon for job appointments in agriculture-related state agencies. Economists tend to be divided between two major blocs according to legitimate professional discrepancies on the path to national development (essentially between those favoring an open economy and those promoting the growth of the internal market). Within these blocs, group loyalties prevail and come to the fore in times of political shifts or job openings. The more technical fields of medicine and petroleum engineering do not display the same intensity of group dynamics. Although pockets of dissension exist, most members are apolitical and more concerned about technical aspects of their professions than about policy in their respective sectors. They share widespread confidence that merit, ability, and hard work pay off in career advancement. Not surprisingly, the professional associations in medicine and engineering most resemble their counterparts in Britain and the United States.

CONCLUSIONS

The Mexican political system is organized in a way that encourages economic growth while moderating redistributive pressures. Most state activity is dedicated to regulating the economy, public security, and information. Complex policy problems in each of these realms require specialized expertise. In the past, professionals' opportunities to affect public policy have been mostly limited to the implementation rather than the formulation stage. To the degree that professionals occupy positions commanding state resources and are entrusted with the task of interpreting official ideology, their influence will increase. Professionals will exercise influence *through* the state as increasingly prominent members of the bureaucratic elite, and not *on* the state as a relatively autonomous force in civil society.

CHAPTER 2

Nationalism
in Mexican Professions

The professions in Mexico experience tension over their degree of nationalism. Partially responsible for solving immense development problems, professionals face overt and subtle pressure to devise Mexican-inspired solutions. The philosophies, technologies and procedures of some professions are more compatible with national norms than are others. Some of the reasons why all Mexican professions cannot be true manifestations of Mexican nationhood are discussed in Chapter 1. Most Mexican professions were late starters and are dependent on foreign technology. The question of professional nationalism is important because its presence or absence is one explanatory factor for the degree of political power professionals can claim in Mexican society. It is not a simple matter, however, to establish the degree of their identification with and contributions to the nation.

Although under pressure and subject to redefinition, Mexican nationalism is not likely to weaken much over the coming decades. Nationalism has been a positive force for national integration and provides a common identity to disparate linguistic, indigenous, and regional groups. It has alleviated class conflict and social tension. The state has benefited from nationalism, disseminated it through the educational system, reinforced it in public ceremonies, and relied on it in designing foreign policy. Nationalism is a constant in Mexican life, affecting all strands of the social fabric. At the same time, no social entity is obliged to be nationalistic. The values of nationalism are not imposed dogmatically; different currents are tolerated. Sometimes the heavy emphasis on nationalism is an artifice, and an individual in a powerful institutional post can manifest varying degrees of fidelity to nationalism, depending on his audience. Yet the influence is so strong and pervasive that it cannot be ignored in the study of the professions, especially since professions have increasingly become international in scope and have difficulty maintaining their national identity.

Some professions, by their very nature, can easily portray themselves as defenders of national norms. Law, for instance, is not a late starter in Mexico. Civil and criminal law, while dependent on the 1917 Constitution, bear a close resemblance to statutes of the nineteenth century and even to the colonial period.[1] The law profession in few countries is dependent on foreign technology, and in Mexico even less so. The juridical system has been highly immune to transplants from abroad, except in the methodology of legal research. Mexican jurists, in fact, consider themselves exporters of innovative legislation in the areas of fiscal incentives for private investment and import substitution. A law degree has commonly been considered a prerequisite for cultured and well-rounded Mexicans, whether or not they practice the profession. Lawyers feel that theirs is the master discipline and the integrator of state and society. The guild believes that law engenders leadership qualities, and its practitioners have the potential to be visionaries. In the modern era, the profession has spawned highly talented individuals who have changed to other careers, where they have become prominent in articulating Mexican nationalism. Examples are Pablo González Casanova (political sociologist), Carlos Fuentes (writer), Rubén Bonifaz Nuño (poet), Daniel Cosío Villegas (historian), and Víctor Flores Olea (educator). Lawyers feel that their legacy has been one of addressing significant social problems, and that their training provides tools and procedures for resolving them.

These claims, however, are increasingly under challenge. The law profession has become more identified with corruption and less involved in public debates concerning justice, welfare, progress, and legitimacy. It is the sociologists, not the lawyers, who observe that Mexico is economically underdeveloped and then ask the question, Where is justice? The nationalistic stature of law in the national hierarchy of professions is elevated, but it is not immutable.

Other professions have more difficulty than does law in affirming their nationalism. Three questions are important in this respect. First, what were the modern origins of the profession?

Does the profession trace its roots to a heroic event, in the Homeric sense, which is imprinted on the national consciousness? Second, has the profession molded foreign technology to national needs and idiosyncracies? Better yet, has it developed indigenous techniques that are well suited to national characteristics, and exported some of them? Third, is the profession engaged in debates of national social and political consequence? Do other groups look to it to help define their own positions, and have its professional perspectives helped set a national debating agenda?

The national-international tension in Mexican professions has been expressed in several ways. Economics is a case of physical division, whereby two relatively well defined groups have emerged with national or international viewpoints on suitable paths to economic development. At the opposite extreme is medicine, which has so internalized an imported approach to health care that dissidents who would propose a more Mexican model are a small minority. Petroleum engineers have creatively preserved the chastity of their discipline (and of their employer, PEMEX or Petróleos Mexicanos), and have resisted seduction by the seven sisters and their technologically exciting cousins, the petroleum service companies. Agronomy, which has grown from very respectable nationalistic roots, witnessed the invention of a modern and powerful technology (a high-yielding wheat variety) within Mexican borders. The irony is that the invention was accomplished by foreigners, and the technology was not easily adaptable by those who were the supposed beneficiaries of the Mexican Revolution. Agronomy, like economics, tends to be split into two groups, with the proponents of a nationalistic approach smaller in number but more vocal.

These four professions can be analyzed according to their nationalistic origins in the modern period, the way in which they adopted or created technology, and their contribution to debates on national development.

PETROLEUM ENGINEERING

The most notable event in the twentieth century for petroleum engineering was on March 18, 1938, when President Lázaro Cárdenas expropriated the foreign oil companies. While some Mexicans had formal training in petroleum engineering prior to expropriation, only a half-dozen Mexicans, working mainly with foreign oil companies, were prepared to assume drilling, exploration, and management functions upon the creation of Petróleos Mexicanos. The petroleum issue in the 1930s was emotional, and the expropriation asserted national sovereignty and self-respect. The measure was immensely popular inside Mexico, and inspired these young petroleum engineers. A spirit of nationalism characterized the profession from its conception, and was reinforced by the ostracization of Petróleos Mexicanos for many years by the large international oil companies.

Engineering has been prominent in Mexican development since the mines of New Spain supplied the mints of the Kingdom of Castilla and Aragón. The first school of mines in Mexico was founded in the eighteenth century, and techniques for extracting silver, gold, lead, mercury, and chrome were developed in Mexico. Mexico traditionally had outstanding professionals in geology and mining engineering. The modern oil industry began near Tampico, Tamaulipas, in 1901. Although the field was U.S.-owned by the Mexican Petroleum Company, it was a Mexican geologist, Ezequiel Ordóñez, who correctly read the structure of the field to extract sufficient oil for commercial purposes.[2] After Ordóñez proved the marketability of Mexican oil, large international oil companies, which were competing for dominance worldwide, including in the United States and Middle East, began widespread drilling in Mexico. The major zone of exploitation was the Golden Lane (*Faja de Oro*), extending from the Río Pánuco on the north border of the state of Veracruz along the coast of Tamaulipas. The major American oil companies involved were Standard Oil of New Jersey, Sinclair, Standard Oil of California, Sábalo, Seaboard, and Cities Service. The British companies owned by Royal-Dutch Shell included 70 percent of the Mexican oil indirectly under the Mexican Eagle (El Aguila) Group.[3]

The discipline of petroleum engineering is a combination of geology, civil engineering, topography, and mechanical engineering. Juan Salvador Agraz, a chemical engineer, developed the curriculum in petroleum engineering at the National School of Engineering between 1928 and 1932. He and a Russian named Iván (Juan) Korzujin examined the course programs at the universities of Oklahoma, California, Texas, Cambridge, Moscow, and the French School of Engineering, merging them appropriately for instruction on the development of Mexican oil reservoirs. At first, there was not much student demand or enrollment in the program. Foreign oil companies preferred to hire their own nationals for engineering work, and the job itself was arduous and located far from city life. In 1932 the Mexican government legislated that the companies were required to employ a certain percentage of Mexican workers; simultaneously, the companies found that they could hire Mexican engineers more cheaply than they could bring foreigners to Mexico, and that the Mexicans had a better feel for the lay of the land and for employee relations.

After March 18, 1938, twelve Mexican professionals formed the core staff of PEMEX and only six were petroleum engineers: Manuel Rodríguez Aguilar, Vicente Fuentes, Jesús de la Garza, Francisco Inguanzo, Miguel Quiros Barranco, and Armando Morán Juárez. Although Rodríguez Aguilar was the oldest and had been working for British Petroleum in Holland at the time, the emergent leader of the group was Francisco Inguanzo, who had just graduated from the National University and worked for Laguna Mexican Oil Company, a British affiliate. This handful of professionals was not prepared to confront the challenges of the petroleum industry, especially in light of the withdrawal of most of the foreign engineers and an embargo on tubes and other inputs from the countries affected by the expropriation. The struggle over technology was waged with a feeling of nationalism. The Mexican pioneers in the field spent part of their time in university teaching, and inculcated a spirit of sacrifice and national dedication in succeeding generations of students. Students who graduated in 1939 went immediately to on-line positions. The pace of work was hectic. One engineer often did the work done by four before expropriation. Normally, one engineer monitors twenty-five artificial well systems; in PEMEX, one engineer needed to monitor one hundred. An engineer who entered PEMEX at this time described the feeling:

> There was mystique around the profession. We felt patriotism for the industry. All of us had a great desire to move ahead, and not fail the trust placed in us . . . All of us wanted to contribute to the triumph of the industry. We were motivated by great enthusiasm despite the difficulties in human resources, equipment, and technology.[4]

Over the years the number of engineers increased, as did their competence. Petroleum technology moved progressively through several stages, and the course curriculum at the National University and Polytechnical Institute kept pace. The methodology for oil exploration in the nineteenth century was qualitative (for example, drilling near salt water, which was often associated with oil). The next step emphasized the geology of rock formations. Then came gravity and magnetic techniques to locate potentially rich deposits. Electrical logging took a profile of the electronic characteristics of the well, without the need for an exhaustive analysis of each core sample. PEMEX offered generous fellowships to encourage enrollment in university programs, and by the 1950s had completely staffed its engineering positions with Mexicans. After the settlement of the outstanding compensation claims in November 1941, commercial trade in oil products and machinery opened with the United States. The companies whose properties were nationalized generally maintained a non-cooperative attitude toward Mexico, in contrast to those industries that provided inputs for oil production. Mexican engineers trained with supplier companies, such as packers, and producers of gelatin, drill bits, electrical logging equipment, and tools. Prominent service companies, such as Halliburton and McCullough, welcomed PEMEX interns.

PEMEX remained very sensitive to preserving its national autonomy, as evidenced by the creation of the Mexican Institute of Petroleum (IMP) and its typical procedures with respect to contracting with foreign companies. The IMP was founded in 1966 to develop and adapt petroleum technology for Mexican needs. Since few Mexican engineers have studied postgraduate programs abroad, the IMP is very much a homegrown institution. In the past, the IMP developed geological and geophysical survey techniques to detect oil and gas-bearing strata. Recently, it has concentrated on off-shore production and drilling platforms with the capacity to drill at enormous depths.[5]

Since the 1940s, PEMEX's bidding process for foreign inputs has been designed to develop Mexican technology. Most foreign companies tendering bids have been from the United States. Petróleos Mexicanos indicates technical specifications, and three to eight companies usually submit bids, including delivery date and budget figures for different line items. These proposals are analyzed for features other than bottom-line cost. When the contract is signed, PEMEX insists that, as the equipment is being built, the winning company accepts the provision to train Mexicans in assembly, operation, and maintenance. The Mexican engineers also visit locations where similar equipment is in use to learn, directly from the operators, of problems likely to arise and how to handle them. PEMEX usually constructs the next installation itself, with little or no foreign engineering inputs. The procedures followed, although somewhat time-consuming and costly, have permitted PEMEX to obtain technology by paying for it just once at what it considers a reasonable price. The strategy has enabled a level of national control over technology used in Mexico, even though it originally was imported.

Many petroleum engineers calculate that, when Mexicans do not participate in installation of the equipment, dependency continues over a long period of time and the cost of technology is much greater. During Jorge Díaz Serrano's administration as general director of PEMEX (1976–1981), a concern arose over the degree of subcontracting to foreign companies. A large number of jobs were contracted under very generous terms for the foreign companies. Differences of opinion pertained to whether PEMEX was purchasing technology in a way consistent with national interests. Practically no petroleum engineer felt that Mexico should develop all its own technology, nor did any believe that Mexico should depend wholly on imports. The policy disagreement was over the way to acquire technology, and issues of cost, length of dependency, and rights to reproduce the technology in Mexico. A number of leading engineers were critical of the rapid expansion of PEMEX infrastructure built by foreign companies.

This debate, even during the Díaz Serrano mandate, was subdued, and petroleum engineers have not assumed prominent positions on issues of national development. Their technical orientation and reliance on the state for employment apparently have impeded their addressing broader national issues, even those that relate directly to their sphere of activity. Thus petroleum engineers freely admit that they "are not very interested in debating policy issues."[6] "I'd say that there really have not been any debates in the profession. There are discussions, perhaps, on certain aspects of the productive process. But there have not been overt discrepancies with government policy."[7] This reluctance to manifest nationalistic viewpoints on petroleum policy means that newer generations of petroleum engineers are not thoroughly socialized in the principles that characterized the profession at its creation. It also means that the government has not seen a need to co-opt a militant petroleum engineering viewpoint by appointing members of the profession to the most senior public sector posts. Since its founding, no petroleum engineer has served as general director of PEMEX.

AGRONOMY

Another profession with links to national symbols is agronomy. An important revolutionary objective was agrarian reform and land distribution. In the Cárdenas period (1936–1940), agronomists were professionally engaged in implementing the agrarian reform in association with topographers and civil engineers. Agronomists who began professional activities at that time were inspired by the prospect of assisting the new *ejido* structure.[8] Over time, however, the profession became more technified. Agronomists dedicated to principles of social justice found little support for their views in the state economic policies, which favored private commercial farmers over the typical *ejido*. A residual feeling of obligation to peasant interests permeates the profession today, and has manifested itself in a group informally referred to as *campesinistas*. The bulk of the profession, however, marches to a different tune, one that stresses high yields with the use of manufactured inputs, much on the model of U.S. agriculture.

Prior to 1890, most of the students at the National Agricultural School in San Jacinto were sons of *hacendados* who, upon completing their studies, returned to administer their fathers' *ranchos*. Agronomy as a profession had very little influence in the social and political direction of the country. After the Revolution, topographers were called upon to create *ejidos* out of agricultural land. During the 1920s and 1930s, agronomists collaborated closely in this process, became actively involved in peasant organization, and were prominent in national politics under the Obregón and Calles presidencies. A veteran agronomist recalled:

> I left school more than fifty years ago. My generation was very close to the 1910 Revolution . . . . Many of us participated in dividing up the land . . . . We felt mystique for the cause of the campesino and the agrarian reform.[9]

The expertise of the agronomist subsequently was compromised by two factors. First, the distribution of land was based more on political than on economic considerations. Much land was allocated to *caciques* (bosses), who concentrated power during the Revolution, and this land, some of it the best in Mexico, remained in private hands. Even the land that was reserved for *ejidos* was not efficiently distributed in terms of productive capacity, and many *ejidos* suffered from poor land/person ratios. Second, the Cárdenas period set the stage for massive irrigation projects as a means of increasing food production. While agronomists were being incorporated into the state budget as public employees, capital infrastructure under the direction of civil engineers absorbed virtually all the sector's budget. Agronomists, who worked in association with the topographers and might have elevated their professional influence in the 1940s, found themselves playing second fiddle to civil engineers during the period of agricultural expansion from 1946 to 1965.[10]

The National Agricultural School of San Jacinto was founded in 1854 in the capital, about 8 kilometers from the zócalo (Mexico City's central square), and in 1923 moved to Chapingo campus, 36 kilometers along the road to Puebla.[11] The training program for a licenciate degree became progressively more specialized in response to the heavy government emphasis on irrigation and the growth of the agricultural sciences. Students could major in irrigation, genetics, parasitology, soils, or agricultural economics. This tendency toward technical specialization helped erode the revolutionary mystique. Several of these approaches, as influenced by international advances in the field, were rarely suited to the poor land and capital assets of the typical *ejido*, whereas they were appropriate to conditions in large-scale privately owned agricultural tracts in the northeast and northwest. During World War II the Secretariat of Agriculture and Livestock signed a technical assistance contract with the Rockefeller Foundation, which brought a number of talented young U.S. genetics researchers to Mexico to further develop existing efforts (such as that of Eduardo Taboada) to increase production. The program also provided fellowships to study in the United States. Approximately three hundred Mexicans received postgraduate degrees in the United States between 1948 and 1972, funded by the Rockefeller and Ford foundations, by the universities themselves, and by other institutions. These studies reinforced the technical competence of Mexican agronomists in an academic ambience that corresponds very little to the agronomic conditions of typical *ejido* producers. Many of these persons later assumed leading positions in the Mexican agricultural sector.

The presence of the foreigners had several ramifications. The first was to demonstrate that agronomy, unlike law or medicine, required getting your hands dirty. At the time Mexican agronomists rarely touched the earth, did fumigations, or took soil samples themselves. The Rockefeller scientists took off their shoes, watered plants, and carried bags of soil, jobs that Chapingo professionals would have left to the peon.

Another influence was to encourage joint research and teaching, somewhat on the model of the U.S. Land Grant College. The Postgraduate College at Chapingo was founded in 1959 on the principle of integrating teaching, research, and extension. The National Institute of Agricultural Research (INIA) was created in 1961, and most of the Rockefeller team (including the future Nobel Prize winner, Norman Borlaug) transferred to it. For many years he and other agricultural scientists had been collaborating to improve wheat varieties in various ecological zones in Mexico. The payoff occurred in a semidwarf variety that increased potential yields on farmers' fields from 4.5 to 9.0 tons per hectare and proved resistant to plagues, toppling, and inclement weather. In 1965, based in part on the astounding successes of the wheat germ plasma improvement program, international donors established, with Mexican approval, the International Maiz and Wheat Improvement Center (CIMMYT) near the Chapingo campus at El Batán. CIMMYT staff absorbed virtually all the long-term Rockefeller resident scientists, who continued their experimentation and dissemination on a worldwide basis.

A nagging concern, however, was that this spectacular invention, which helped avert famine in many parts of Asia, proved unattractive to Mexican farmers, especially those to whom revolutionary promises had not been kept. Those *ejidos* and small farmers who never benefited from large-scale irrigation and state credit policies could not afford the fertilizers, pesticides, and other inputs required for the new varieties to be effective. This historical quirk was not the fault of the foreign scientists. Nevertheless, the profession of agronomy had evolved in such a way that its major technological breakthrough did little to reassert its claims to nationalism, at least to the degree that nationalism in the agricultural sector was coterminus with the agrarian policies of the Cárdenas presidency.

In response, beginning in the mid-1970s, a sub-group of agronomists (joined by other professionals) began to elaborate a different function for the profession, which placed the campesino squarely in the middle of professional attention. Called the *campesinistas*, this minority was less intrigued with raising the threshold of optimal yields on the best land and more concerned with improving the farming system of typical poor peasants in various ecological zones.[12] Academically, *campesinistas* conducted research on on-farm and off-farm labor, unbalanced markets, local power structures, informal credit arrangements, agronomic practices, erosion and other kinds of ecological deterioration, as well as on higher yielding corn, bean, and wheat varieties that could be tended with inputs within the peasants' financial reach. Politically, *campesinistas* vociferously urged a shift in state priorities from large-scale capital-intensive farming to subsidies and supports for poor farmers who produce basic grains.

Agronomists infrequently have been appointed to top policy-making positions in Mexico. When such an event occurs, the representative of the profession has come invariably from the modernizing, rather than from the *campesinista*, wing of the field.

ECONOMICS

The first generation of modern economic policymakers was trained as lawyers and had an intuitive feeling for economics. They emerged in the wake of the Cárdenas period, and devised practical and innovative policies for Mexican industrial development during World War II. As economics became more sophisticated internationally, a bifurcation emerged in the discipline at home. Promising young economists increasingly went abroad for graduate training. Those who studied in the United States tended to return with an appreciation for macroeconomic policy tools, which relied on quantitative methods. Their neoclassical approach to policy proved to be compatible with the approach of Mexican financiers and industrialists, and they rose rapidly in the public sector. Those economists who studied first at the National School of Economics (ENE, or Escuela Nacional de Economía) and later went to Europe for postgraduate training tended to promote nationalistic policies that would protect Mexican industry and increase the size of the internal market. Today the two groups are fairly evenly matched and both are accommodated within the diversified Mexican public sector.

The Bank of Mexico, founded in 1925, did not establish a tradition in economics in its early years. From the late 1930s to the late 1960s it was directed by a sequence of nonorthodox central bankers, among them Eduardo Villaseñor and Rodrigo Gómez. Villaseñor dabbled in economics at the University of London, studied philosophy, engineering and law at UNAM, and was general director from 1940 to 1945. Gómez started as a clerk in the Bank of México in 1933, obtained no graduate degree, and capped his career as general director from 1952 to 1970. These individuals, who were born at the turn of the century, were not terribly knowledgeable about modern economics and were not guided by any specific economics philosophy. Exposed to the misery of the Great Depression, they were aware that Mexico's economy was underdeveloped. Although nationalistic and members of the Cárdenas generation, they were not radicals but action-oriented generalists. During World War II they experienced difficulty obtaining capital goods from the United States. Thus they were convinced of the need to industrialize Mexico, and they chose import substitution as the means to achieve this objective. Excellent politicians, they were skillful at designing legislation and understanding market conditions. They worked in close association with local Mexican industrialists, especially those in CANACINTRA. The *desarrollo estabilizador* model was the culmination of their work.[13] However, they never mastered or employed sophisticated economic policy-making tools.

While generalists occupied the top positions in the Bank of Mexico, Treasury, and Nacional Financiera, a younger group filled technical and advisory roles.[14] When the Bank of Mexico initiated its foreign study program in the 1940s, this younger group averaged about 25 years old, and many traveled to the United States and England for graduate degrees. Víctor Urquidi went to the London School of Economics; Octaviano Campos Salas to the University of Chicago; Raúl Salinas to Harvard and Washington universities; and Raúl Ortiz Mena to Harvard University. Others, including Alfonso Pulido Islas, remained in Mexico and became more deeply involved in consolidating the National School of Economics.[15] The orientation of those who studied in Europe tended to bear some resemblance to the teachings at ENE of the National University.

The licenciate program at UNAM never stressed economics or business administration as much as it did political economy. Its curriculum was structured around historical and social themes, with a secondary emphasis on instrumental and technical aspects of economics. The economics section of the Faculty of Law was founded in 1929 by Narciso Bassols, a Mexican revolutionary of the 1920s who authored the agricultural law of 1927. He was joined by others who saw value in a systematic study of the economy, including the lawyer Daniel Cosío Villegas, the banker Enrique González Aparicio, the anthropologist Miguel Othón de Mendizábal, the agronomist Manuel Meza, the businessman Pablo Macedo, and the self-taught intellectual Jesús Silva Herzog. Formal economics training did not compete well with law, however, and when the ENE was formed as a separate unit in 1935 few students enrolled. The popularity of the program grew gradually, but even in the 1940s enrollment never exceeded three hundred. The professors were essentially self-taught, and earned their livelihoods mainly as functionaries in the public bureaucracy.

From 1929 to 1961 the most respected teachers were not full-time educators but men who had distinguished themselves in public service.[16] Ramón Beteta, Antonio Carillo Flores, Gilberto Loyo, Eduardo Bustamante, Emigdio Martínez Adame, and Mario Souza were first and foremost public officials who viewed the School as a means to strengthen a political constituency in the management of the state. A typical figure in the development of the ENE was Horacio Flores de la Peña. Born in 1923, he studied at UNAM under Eduardo Bustamante (Secretary of National Properties), did graduate studies in economics at Washington University, and worked at ILPES in Santiago, Chile. Flores de la Peña was not a scholarly economist, but was a close associate of Michal Kalecki and Joan Robinson at Cambridge University, and Cambridge economics characterized his thinking. As a professor at ENE, its director in 1966, and Secretary of National Properties from 1970 to 1974, Flores de la Peña instructed and recruited a large number of economists into upper-level public sector positions.

Meanwhile, neoclassical economics was building strength through the return of large numbers of economists who had studied at U.S. universities with the aid of central bank scholarships. Newly created Mexican undergraduate and graduate programs emerged with an orientation toward quantitative methods and neoclassical economics. Economics programs at the Autonomous University of Guadalajara, the Monterrey Institute of Technology, Anáhuac, Iberoamerican University, and the Autonomous Technological Institute of Mexico (ITAM) all developed curricula more similar to neoclassical and monetarist economics than to political economy. These institutions recruited students from a higher social class than did the ENE, and did not deliberately transmit a sense of social consciousness, which was the basis of the ENE program. The private university graduates knew statistics, regression curves, and mathematics, spoke English, and were relatively unconcerned about the externalities of their equations. Furthermore, the university crisis of 1965 resulted in the resignation of Flores de la Peña and the capture of ENE by Marxist economists with no interest whatsoever in quantitative methods. While useful for social criticism and rhetoric, the School's effectiveness in teaching practical problem-solving methodologies declined considerably, and graduates increasingly discovered little demand for their skills, among either state or private sector employers.

By the early 1970s two discernible currents had developed in the economics profession in Mexico. One school of thought can be described as nationalistic state capitalist, while the other has been more aligned with neoclassical theory. A third group, the Marxist intellectuals, is influential in teaching programs at ENE (and other public universities), but it does not represent a force in the profession in terms of institutionalized state power.

The nationalists believe in state intervention in the economy, an increase in public expenditures, and a larger role for public enterprises. Left of center, these economists have tried to interpret Mexico's economic dilemmas from a historical perspective. They often speak of economics in sociological terms, such as group alliances, national independence, and the dominant influence of the business class. They conclude that Mexico is a colonized country in transition to a developed state. Its best possible future is noncapitalistic, and the development path should be as close to socialism as possible. Since there are insufficient social forces pushing in that direction, they refer to an *economía de transición,* or mixed economy. On specific policies, the group believes that public expenditure should be increased and state enterprises should expand, whether or not they make a profit. They do not rule out contact with U.S. corporations, but are suspicious of transnationals and would be happier with less U.S. direct investment in Mexico. On monetary questions, they would tolerate more inflation if it brought greater industrial growth. On trade policy, they prefer higher tariffs and greater self-reliance, which in financial terms translate into lowered interest rates to encourage expansion of middle-sized industry, with a positive effect on employment.[17]

The neoclassical approach in the profession is oriented toward monetarism, free trade, and private initiative; it falls to the right of center along the Mexican political spectrum. This group is not interested in historical or global interpretations, but in pragmatic instruments for short-term economic management. The government's responsibilities are to stimulate savings, capital investment, plant modernization, and assure that the price system functions. In this way the country can plan its future as do other developed countries, relying heavily on the private financial system. The group believes that public sector expansion is disadvantageous; while not rejecting the existence of public enterprises, it believes their products should be priced at market levels and not subsidized. As for controls on foreign investment, these economists say that Mexico can and should use U.S. capital for development, always endeavoring to extract the maximum benefit for Mexico from the relationship. On agrarian issues, they advocate devising efficient means of using the land, with a tacit preference for owner-operated middle-sized holdings rather than the traditional *ejido.* While they might agree that more tax revenue is needed, they feel that money is spent inefficiently in the public sector, partially because of a lack of accountability. They sympathize with the private sector, which urges the government to expunge corruption before increasing taxes.[18]

It would be misleading to draw these lines too boldly and thus convey caricatures of the two positions. On many issues there is no real difference between the two schools of thought. They have similar viewpoints on income and salary policies and fiscal reform, and neither group wants to squander Mexican oil reserves. No economist has in mind establishing greater external dependency. Often the differences become clear more in the policy questions that each group asks than in its answers. The solutions, however, have divergent ideological implications. One group believes that industrialization and democracy will be achieved by strengthening private enterprise, reducing the role of the state, and returning to free trade. Other economists believe that to achieve those goals the state has to redistribute income, shelter the poor, and create jobs.

Until 1976, advocates of the two groups were spread about more or less randomly in the state's financial institutions; during the López Portillo administration, state agencies became more closely identified with each position. Virtually all of the senior economics civil servants in the Echeverría and López Portillo governments trained in the Bank of Mexico as young professionals, mainly during the restrictive monetary policies of Antonio Ortiz Mena, who was Secretary of Hacienda from 1958 to 1970. Those who found these policies compatible with their training and ideology tended to see their careers advance in institutions whose functions in the financial system were more restrictive than expansionist. These agencies were the Treasury, Programming and Budgeting, and the Bank of Mexico. Under López Portillo, these institutions were headed for a considerable length of time by David Ibarra (trained at Stanford University), Miguel de la Madrid (Harvard University), and Romero Kolbek (the Mexican private banking system). For others, the Bank of Mexico did not produce an indelible stamp; Horacio Flores de la Peña and Javier Alejo rejected the Banco de Mexico's restrictive orientation, and were not promoted within its ranks. They found Nacional Financiera and SEPAFIN (Secretariat of Industries) more congenial to their viewpoints, and under the Echeverría government experimented with more expansionist policies. The successor political generation, including Carlos Tello and José Andrés de Oteyza, also advocated more nationalistic, expansionist economic policies. The results were mixed. Oteyza, as Secretary of Industries, struggled constantly to promote middle-sized national industries against the steady advances of large national and multinational firms, while Carlos Tello was forced to resign his post when he argued excessively with the then-Secretary of Hacienda, Julio Moctezuma Cid. He later reemerged prominently during the 1982 private bank nationalization.

Most insiders recognize the existence of the two currents, and their symbiotic relationship within the same bureaucracy. In the words of one:

> Today monetarists and anti-monetarists seem to concentrate in one or another sector. But this is something less than a 'split.' These economists have to communicate.[19]

Others observed:[20]

> The conservative and statist currents coexist . . . . These groups
> come together as an operational mafia within the government.
> Often the leftist economist who has become rich begins to defend
> rightist positions, and leftists have to soften their lines to survive in
> the bureaucracy . . . . There have been cabinet crises involving this
> split. It was very clear when Carlos Tello confronted Moctezuma
> Cid's stability bias. Both had to leave. So the lesson is that the two
> currents coexist and they come into conflict. If the conflict is too
> strong, their spokesmen are kicked out.

More than other social scientists, economists frequently
justify the worth of their knowledge on its practical applications,
and Mexican economists from the nationalistic current have been
somewhat successful in promoting policies and ideas pertinent to
Mexican and Latin American development problems. Origins for
the policies of import substitution can be found in the research
and writing of the Bank of Mexico in the 1940s, where Raúl
Prebisch resided after being dismissed from the Argentine Central
Bank. This policy was first applied in Mexico and later, through
the work of CEPAL, it characterized economic development
policies throughout Latin America. In the early 1950s the writing
of Juan Francisco Noyola was widely respected as an original
contribution to the study of inflation. He was one of the first to
attribute inflation to structural rigidities in the economy (such as
an unproductive agricultural sector, owing to *latifundios*), and
more well known social scientists, such as Osvaldo Sunkel and
Fernando Henrique Cardoso, credit him with having influenced
their thinking.[21] Noyola was killed in an airplane accident in 1962
while advising the Cuban government.

The more modern generation of economists, especially those
trained in neoclassical theory, boasts only a few researchers
making original contributions to the field. Many of the
practitioners' ideas on the international economic order come
from the occasional papers of the IMF, the World Bank, and the
OECD. In great part these persons have studied at U.S.
universities, know the international journal literature better than
Latin American writings, and often have had professional
experience in Washington at the Bretton Woods institutions.
They typically find the practical economic summaries of New
York money market banks more useful than *Trimestre Económico*,
published in Mexico City. One public sector economist, trained
on the Continent, questioned the validity of some of these
approaches.

The neoclassical economists have gone abroad for graduate degrees, often at excellent universities. They know how to manage sophisticated techniques, which they never question. Their theoretical instruction has been insufficient because economic theory may be inappropriate for social reality in Mexico. It is a fact that economics students from Chicago, Harvard, and Berkeley, although terribly competent, do not have the theory to deal with Mexico's problems. We are talking about underdevelopment. The profession's cumulative knowledge is running behind social reality.[22]

While the criticism of neoclassical economics may be well-taken, it would be a mistake to assume that nationalistic state capitalism is more applicable. The significance of the two schools is the flexibility they give Mexican political leadership to switch from one set of policies to those diametrically opposed, in the confidence that both have legitimate professional defenders.

MEDICINE

Medicine, like law, is one of the original liberal professions in Mexico that has maintained its importance in the modern era. Medicine experienced a significant change, however, in the 1940s when its orientation became less clinical and more individualist and biological. The profession began to follow medical practices established in the United States and broke its ties with the French school. Neither revolutionary imperatives nor nationalistic symbols provoked this transformation. Although the nation's leading doctors tend to be employees of public health institutions (IMSS, SSA, ISSSTE, PEMEX, SDN), medical treatment is curative, pharmaceutically-based and specialized.[23] The majority of doctors working for the state also have private practices. Advocates of clinical medicine gradually are retiring from practice, and virtually no doctors, including the homeopaths, are sympathetic to Mexico's heritage of medicinal herbs and traditional healers (*curanderos*).[24] The conventional medical profession conducts little research, does not subscribe to Mexican medical journals, is apolitical, and is not generally engaged in debating issues of health policy in the country.

The principal foreign influence on the development of medical education in the late nineteenth and early twentieth century was European, especially French. Before 1940, students chose their professional specialization in preparatory school, and those who opted for the biological sciences took their courses in the French language. Premedical students needed to read French fluently before entering university, and professors of medicine typically did their post-graduate degree in Paris. The French medical tradition at the time was clinical and generalist-oriented rather than specialist-oriented. It was taught in Mexico by such persons as Arquelino Villanueva, Ignacio Chávez, and Abraham Ayala González. The doctors investigated the patient's illness as a detective might. After taking a thorough medical history, they would uncover clues using their hands, nose, eyes, and ears. Through palpation and tactile probing, doctors were able to diagnose pneumonia, cancer, and heart disease. Doctors handled a range of about twenty drugs in different combinations. Writing exact prescriptions was an art and was heavily emphasized in school.

Four events transformed diagnostic and therapeutic techniques in Mexico.[25] First, when France was invaded by Nazi Germany in 1940 French textbooks no longer were available to Mexican medical students. They switched to American textbooks and had to learn English. Second, U.S. doctors were conscripted into the war effort, leaving a vacuum to be filled in U.S. hospitals. Persons such as Salvador Zubirán encouraged medical students to do their residency in the United States. Hundreds of Mexican doctors, virtually a whole generation, received advanced training in U.S. hospitals between 1943 and 1946. Third, penicillin was introduced into Mexico in 1944, thus lowering the need for apothecary skills among doctors. Fourth, the IMSS was founded in 1943 as the first state medical institution. These events formed the basis for modern medicine in Mexico, and only the fourth bore any relation to principles of nationalism or revolutionary commitment.

The introduction of U.S. medicine signaled the eclipse of the general practitioner well versed in clinical techniques. Specialization, which was gaining momentum in the United States, also became predominant in Mexico, and Mexican doctors concentrated on one or another subfield, such as cardiology, pathology, hematology, anesthesiology, obstetrics, endocrinology, and pediatrics. Up to and including the contemporary period, the emphasis on specialization has deflected professional attention from preventive medicine and public health toward individual medicine. Some medical leaders in Mexico feel that the profession misadopted the U.S. concept of specialization (which first requires a generalist stage) by directly training specialists in fields beyond the practical needs of Mexican society.

The pharmaceutical revolution substituted the *Physicians Desk Reference* for the guide to apothecary medicine, and produced a new linch-pin in the profession—the drug salesman. No longer was the doctor a *gran señor* who controlled the destinies of lives, and he abdicated his role as a family counsellor. Once he started prescribing brand name drugs, he ceased writing ceremoniously on a piece of paper in poor handwriting a prescription which no one, except the druggist, could read. His elegant vocabulary and hieroglyphics became archaic. A doctor noted that the profession "lost its magic ingredient . . . . Now a person can go into a store and buy medicine like a shirt."[26]

These trends have permeated the medicine practiced in the large state institutions. The Mexican Social Security Institute (IMSS) was founded in 1943 as a response to the 1917 constitutional directive that the state should provide adequate health care to the population. The idea of social medicine had existed in Mexico since the Revolution, but had not been acted upon. The creation of IMSS was resisted by traditional doctors trained in the French tradition, who feared that medicine would become bureaucratized; by industrialists and employers who resented that the government was charging them a third of the cost of the system; and by some unions, who objected to payroll deductions for the services and protested with placards reading *inseguridad social*. The IMSS was welcomed by many young doctors, who were beginning their practices in the 1940s and needed steady employment, especially since the state job did not proscribe their engaging in private practice on the side. Although some of the original doctors were of mediocre quality, improvement was progressive. As IMSS matured, it recruited better doctors through high salaries, better work organization, sophisticated equipment, and trained support staff. The IMSS's reputation grew, as did its coverage (to about a third of the national population). Other state medical institutions are the clinics and hospitals of the Secretariat of Health (whose budget per capita has traditionally—until the De la Madrid government—been one sixth that of the IMSS), ISSSTE (for state employees), and PEMEX and Ferrocarriles Nacionales (for the petroleum and railroad workers, respectively).[27]

Supporters and critics of social medicine in Mexico concede that it is bureaucratic, imbuing its medical professionals with an uncommitted attitude toward work. Doctors complain of a rudimentary doctor/patient relationship, overwork, and conflict with administrators. Typical comments are:

> In some places doctors have to treat forty patients per day and they can't practice correct medicine. After one month, as you can imagine, they are already tired of medicine. They ask one or two

questions in their office, and recommend aspirins on the first go-around. Later they may find out that it is a brain tumor, but it is too late. This situation negates the essence of the medical profession.[28]

In the IMSS, it is very common for doctors to consider the patient to be the enemy. The patient in turn sees the doctor in a bad light, as indifferent, hurried, and trying to finish his work shift.[29]

(More than by the workload) doctors become enraged by medical authorities who do not understand their point of view. Institute directors are always worried about political considerations, not about the service provided to the patients . . . . Some authorities want to control and manipulate the doctors. This brings doctors into conflict with their superiors.[30]

Many doctors start thinking of retirement the day they enter IMSS. This is the epitome of bureaucratism.[31]

While reliable statistics are not available, it is widely believed that a large proportion of doctors working in the state institutions practice their profession also in some other capacity.[32] Those who hold a purported full-time position in more than one state institution are considered least ethical, in that they cut off hours at the tail end of their first shift in one institution, and arrive late for the beginning of their next shift in another institution. On the other hand, no formal objections are raised about doctors who maintain private practices outside the hours of their institutional assignments. Moonlighting doctors justify these multiple jobs on the relatively low remunerations, especially as compared to their U.S. counterparts.

These patterns, combined with their relative lack of organization (discussed in Chapter 4), result in apolitical attitudes. Mexican doctors are not much involved in questions of national health policy. Their political activity tends to concentrate on working conditions within state institutions. Even the intensity of workplace grievances is mollified by the ability to escape to one's private practice in the afternoon or evening. A university-based doctor comments:

If you talk with doctors and oblige them to define their position on health policy, they tend to come out on the Right. If you put the mainstream of Mexican doctors on a political spectrum, they would fall much closer to the beliefs of the American Medical Association than on the side of public health. Doctors recognize that they are salaried workers but they do not accept that label.[33]

Another doctor adds:

> Doctors don't know the difference between health and medicine.
> They think that doctors have responsibility for the nation's health,
> but they don't see that health is linked to jobs, roads, housing, water,
> and schooling . . . . The doctors think that people have a right to
> health, but if you ask them what that means, they don't know. Ask
> a doctor, Do all Mexicans have the right to health? He will say yes.
> Then ask him, Do all Mexicans have the right not to get sick? He
> won't understand what you are talking about.[34]

NATIONALISM VERSUS INTERNATIONALISM

Mexican professions often display a discernible split between
nationalist and internationalist orientations. Law remains most
embedded in national norms and structures, yet increasingly its
spokesmen have abdicated responsibility for contributing
constructively to debates on the nation's future. As the definition
of the Mexican nation changes, lawyers are likely to continue to
slip in prestige. Unless they are able to spearhead that redefinition,
other types of professionals will supplant them in national
leadership roles. In terms of nationalistic identification, the
practices of the medical profession in Mexico are consistent with
international trends (especially those in the United States) and
seem inconsistent with health needs of the majority of the
population. Although the modern manifestations of the Mexican
medical profession began to emerge in the postrevolutionary
period, the model was inspired from abroad and was not created
by the doctors in response to revolutionary challenges. Of all the
professional groups studied in this chapter, medical personnel are
most muted in their public views on issues of national
importance, even those in the health field. The contradiction is
that doctors preserve the greatest social prestige among
professionals in Mexico, despite their apparent apathy toward
nationalistic concerns.

Petroleum engineering, economics, and agronomy have had
different experiences in promoting and/or accommodating
nationalism within their ranks. All three professions entered the
modern period during national consolidation after the Revolution,
with the first most closely associated with a decisive nationalistic
act—the expropriation of the foreign petroleum companies. The
sophisticated nature of petroleum engineering and Mexico's
relatively late start in the field would have predicted a rapid
erosion of nationalistic autonomy faced with obligatory

technological dependency. While erosion appears to be occurring, it is taking place at a relatively slow pace. The memory of the sacrifices of PEMEX's first generation of petroleum engineers sustains the consciousness of the profession. Nationalistic precepts have been internalized in bidding procedures for the purchase of foreign technology, which protect and enhance national independence. Petroleum engineers, however, have been reluctant to contribute to national policy debate, and discussions within the profession tend to revolve around narrow technical concerns.

The agronomic profession is heavily dependent on state employment. Agronomists, who never achieved national stature, have adjusted to their predicament by responding more to the dictates of the state than to the needs of peasant clients, whose interests revolutionary faithfuls would have them serve. State investment in infrastructure, credit, and price supports has favored commercial farmers and agricultural industrialists more than *ejidos* and small farmers, and agronomists have allowed their profession to be molded in like fashion. A countermovement has survived in the profession, tracing its ethical and ideological roots to the revolutionary period. Agricultural modernizers, many of whom have been trained abroad, appear nonetheless to be capable of rejecting the challenge of *campesinistas*, who may have begun their campaign too late. The rapid migration to the cities, the entry of commercial farmers into the production of basic grains, and the dismantling of the *ejidos'* protective legislation during the López Portillo government may remove both the clientele (the peasantry) and its organizational form (the *ejido*) from the purview of agronomic concerns.[35] Should this occur, nationalists within the profession will need to discover new ways to mold the profession in a way that corresponds to particularly Mexican rather than international currents in the field.

Economics is the Mexican profession most clearly divided between nationalists and internationalists, and today appears to be the most lively of those treated here. Spokesmen for each group have developed and refined their positions in formalized training programs, and have even been able to divvy up the public sector bureaucracy. Each defends a different clientele in civil society and has contributed to an ongoing national debate on the preferred path to national development. While the Mexican political system might be indifferent to the nationalism of the agronomic or medical professions, it is unlikely to allow the division in economics to be healed. The positions taken by each side imply different public policies; by adopting one and then another, the state can help achieve equilibrium in the system and attend sequentially to powerful economic actors with divergent interests.

Professional nationalism is one of the important aspects of Mexican professions that separates them from their counterparts in Europe and the United States.[36] Another is their relative tolerance to the expansion of their ranks and their relative inability to regulate training. Entry into the professions is not governed by the university, licensing board, or the professional association, but by the marketplace after the professional degree is awarded.

CHAPTER 3

The Role of University Education in Professional Training

Education plays an important, although not exclusive, role in qualifying individuals to enter a profession. Before the Industrial Revolution, such training took place in the practitioner's office or workshop and the students were called apprentices. Detailed legislation governed the reciprocal obligations of master and apprentice. The system provided rudimentary guarantees that new generations of specialists in the field would be competent. It also assured that the marketplace would not be flooded, in that a craftsman could maintain only as many apprentices as he could afford and keep busy. In the United States and Europe, the nineteeth-century university became the main arena for the transfer and reproduction of professional knowledge in law, engineering, and medicine. The professional guilds supported university training for new members so long as they could influence the curriculum and retain the right of certification. Indeed, fields aspiring to the rank of profession viewed the creation of a degree-granting program at a leading university as an important goal, since this step legitimated its professional activity. The university, thus, served as a partner in the profession's aspirations for high prestige and remuneration.[1] By conducting research and training in advanced methods, the university raised the competence level of young professionals. By requiring extended study without remuneration, it limited the number of aspirants to professional degrees and, thereby, the number of professionals ultimately competing in the marketplace for the same clientele. The university helped reinforce the elite status of the professions.

In Mexico the state, not the profession, has assigned a function to professional training. The university, not the profession, has established the criteria for certifying formal professional competence. The professions have achieved a measure of influence over the marketplace by controlling entry-level employment decisions in some large public and private sector institutions. Their guardianship of the professional ranks, however, comes at the end of the process. Professional groups have not managed (and often have not tried) to achieve a balance between the supply of certified professionals and demand for their services.

State officials need trained specialists for their own employ, and recognize that the economy will not advance without improved expertise in various technical fields. The Secretariat of Public Education frequently plots the need for professionals, and encourages entry into understaffed specialties and discourages entry into others. This sort of educational planning is not pursued tenaciously, however, in part because professional education serves purposes other than producing qualified lawyers, doctors, engineers, or architects.

In an economy in which the GNP grows faster than new employment creation and aspirations for social mobility among popular groups are acute, university training can provide the illusion of personal advancement. The prestige of the title *profesionista* acts as a magnet to the university, which is then delegated the task of overseeing large numbers of young persons during a biological stage of high physical energy. The classroom focuses the attention of socially mobile young adults on books and debate, which is less threatening to stability than alternative pastimes, such as worker organization.[2] It is immaterial that only a small portion will be adequately trained and successful in locating a position related to learned skills. The state finds it cheaper to build a classroom and hire a teacher than to construct a factory. Many persons called university students in Mexico could as easily be classified as the hidden unemployed.

FOUR ACTORS

The current status of professional education and certification can be analyzed in terms of the apparent objectives of four actors and their relative weight in the political equation. The relevant groups are the students, the state, the university, and the professions.[3]

First are the undergraduate students at publicly supported universities who aspire to successful careers through professional training. The universe of students is potentially very large and their economic status low. Relatively lax enrollment procedures allow large numbers to matriculate. Surveys of entering students at UNAM document their low economic position. In 1977, for example, 78.6 percent of UNAM's 271,266 students came from families with total income of less than 8,000 pesos (US$ 355) per month.[4] A large number need to find part-time employment to maintain themselves. The small amount of time available for study and the generally poor secondary school education depresses academic quality. Classes are large and professors are hired on an hourly basis. Students apply pressure to keep homework light and examinations easy. Meanwhile, they try to build friendships and alliances with professors, with other students, or with hirers, which will result in a job upon completing their degrees. Often this strategy requires engaging in political activity supportive of the PRI. A minority is committed to completing the degree and maximizing learning during the university years. The majority's preference is open enrollment and loose standards.

The state genuinely desires highly qualified professionals for public employment. It does not view the national university system, however, as the only means of obtaining this expertise. Large budgetary outlays to universities and university departments on the basis of student enrollment, rather than on the number of graduates, demonstrate that quality or narrowly conceived productivity are not the state's only motives.

The most important function of the university is to provide a channel of expression for young adults from the popular sectors with visions of upward mobility. To achieve this goal, the state keeps university enrollment high and subsidizes a large number of universities, often only at the minimum level required to keep their doors open. The advantages are multiple. First, lower-class youth at least have the chance to attend the university; occasionally an outstanding individual beats the odds, rises up through the system, and makes important contributions to the technical development of Mexico. Second, large universities provide a home for potentially unruly intellectuals. Instead of engaging in direct political action, either as part of the Right or more commonly the Left, these elites are secluded and easily monitored on university campuses. Their criticisms are limited to the written or spoken word, which are tempered by the job security and perquisites of state employment.[5] Third, the system does not deny the state or the economy the number of trained professionals they need for maintenance, reproduction, and growth. These students either come from more wealthy backgrounds and pay fees at private universities, or they are among the graduates of the public universities who pass examinations held by companies and state agencies, which filter out all but the most talented individuals.

The large numbers of students who matriculate and complete their coursework but who do not locate suitable employment in their fields are not casualties of the education system as much as they are successes for the political system. They enter professional training programs with prestige and economic motivations in mind, and satisfy themselves with the symbolic luster of having attended university. As long as they do not rebel, either at the university or afterwards, the university performs a major function for the state, although at considerable financial cost.[6]

University teachers and officials can be divided roughly between two groups. On the one hand are veterans, who recognize that professional education does not have the same function today as it did when they completed their degrees; on the other are idealistic young professors, often trained abroad, who have a clear academic vocation. They attempt to maintain their professional élan and commitment under trying circumstances, often commiserating about what should be. In programs where "massification" has reached gargantuan proportions and efforts to maintain high academic standards are unavailing, university staff goals are displaced and other attitudes prevail. Professors place emphasis on objectives that have little to do with teaching: they seek to obtain research positions without classroom responsibilities; use their university affiliation to increase their fees in private professional practice; recruit students into alliances useful for their career advancement in the university or the state bureaucracy; become outspoken critics of the system in order to garner national or international recognition; or exploit the privileges of tenure and university autonomy to draw a salary with minimal work. University coherence is continuously threatened by those who seek academic goals and by those who accept and support the system-maintenance goals of the academy. Conflict between the two frequently erupts.[7] Except in certain institutes with worldclass scientific leadership, the academically oriented invariably lose or are forced to compromise their values. Although often supported by leading members of the profession, they cannot combat successfully the combined pressures of the students and the state.

Speaking privately, many professional leaders would prefer to raise university entrance requirements, restrict the number of students, concentrate scattered resources on creating superior training programs, and match the number of jobs with an equal number of highly qualified university graduates. Their influence on university policies, however, usually is nil. These leaders lack the ability to change current trends, primarily because of the low cohesion of the professional associations and their lack of legitimacy in certifying new entrants into the professions, compared with the weight of segments of the faculty, the students, and the state. Moreover, while the prevailing situation may be unfortunate, it does have compensations. The number of professionals grows without directly challenging the earning power of those who have already begun their careers. High enrollments ratify the status of the profession in the society at large. Young students bestow prestige on established professionals, who enjoy eminence in their eyes. Practicing professionals help their employers design job examinations, analogous to certification tests, which exclude the wholly incompetent. Finally, despite wastage, the system produces the number of proficient graduates needed to expand and enhance the ranks. Professionals thus have not mounted their defense at the doors of the university as the place to control entry into the professions. Rather, they have positioned themselves increasingly at the gates of the workplace, where they help choose the graduating students who will be gainfully employed.

The motivations of the individuals and institutions described above are variables that apply to Mexican professions in differing degrees. The professions can be analyzed according to the presence, preponderance, or absence of certain variables. The most significant are (a) the scale of university enrollment, (b) the quality of teaching programs, (c) the graduation/matriculation ratio, (d) the existence of high-tuition elite institutions, (e) the degree of emphasis on post-graduate training abroad, (f) the use of preemployment examinations, and (g) the existence of post-hire schools to teach deficient technical skills.

The value assigned to all these variables is not the same for each profession, which helps explain the evolution of university education in each field. Table 1 offers quantitative and qualitative data pertaining to the five professions under study. Analysis of this table shows that enrollments are high in each of the professions, except petroleum engineering, and that matriculation/graduation ratios are low. Schools have proliferated in all fields but petroleum engineering. The public and private sectors have inserted a control on access to employment by obliging job aspirants in some fields to take special examinations. Elite training institutions have emerged in medicine and economics, and post-graduate training has become *de rigueur* in economics and

Table 1 University Degree Programs, Enrollment, Graduates, and Unemployment in Selected Professions

	Medicine	Law	Economics	Agronomy	Petroleum Engineering	Architecture	Civil Engineering
Year of Founding of First University Program[a]	1833	1553	1935	1854	1915	1786	1868
Nationwide officially recognized degree-granting programs[b]	46	62	41	38	2	47	58
Nationwide licenciate degree enrollment[b]	92,275	59,970	22,107	36,333	914	29,059	30,921
Sample ratio of ingresados/egresados/titulados[c]	2.5/ 1.4/ 1	3.1/ 1.9/ 1	4.4/ 2.9/ 1	5.8/ 3.3/ 1	19.7/ 1.2/ 1	3.1/ 1.7/ 1	4.8/ 1.7/ 1
Existence of public sector qualifying exam prior to employment[d]	Yes – 90% failure rate for residency in state hospitals	No	Yes – 67% failure rate at Bank of Mexico	Yes – 45% failure rate at INIA	Yes – 10% failure rate at PEMEX; 80% at IMP.	No	No

| Estimated number of unemployed professionals[d] | 15,000 | High | High | Negligible but looming large | None | Negligible | Negligible |

---

[a]Unión de Universidades de América Latina, *Censo universitario latinoamericano 1966-1969* (Mexico City: Secretaría General, 1971). The first program in each field was located at UNAM, except for agronomy, founded at ENA in Chapingo.

[b]Data for 1980; see ANUIES, *Anuario estadístico 1980* (Mexico City: Asociación Nacional de Universidades e Institutos de Enseñanza Superior, 1981). The information for petroleum engineering was supplemented from Interview No. 28.

[c]An *ingresado* is a matriculated student, an *egresado* one who has completed all coursework for the licenciate degree, and a *titulado* one who has passed the qualifying examination (*examen profesional*) and completed the thesis, if required. The ratios for medicine, law, economics, architecture, and civil engineering pertain to the UNAM entering classes of 1971, 1972, and 1973, and to the Autonomous University of Nuevo León entering classes of 1973 and 1974. The petroleum engineering statistics pertain to the UNAM entering classes of 1971, 1972, and 1973. The agronomy statistics pertain to the Nuevo León entering classes of 1973 and 1974, and the ENA entering classes of 1966 through 1975. Statistics on the academic history of entering classes is difficult to obtain; few universities compile them and available data are not centrally located. These figures allow the entering class five years to become *egresados*, and another year to become *titulados*. In theory, each of these licenciate programs should be completed in five years. Sources are: ANUIES, *La enseñanza superior en México 1970-1976* (Mexico City: Secretaría General Ejecutiva, 1976), pp. 150-156; Universidad Nacional Autónoma de México, *Anuario Estadístico* (Mexico City: Secretaría General de Servicios Auxiliares, 1971-1980); Universidad Autónoma de Nuevo León, *Universidad en cifras* (Monterrey: Dirección de Planeación Universitaria, 1980-1981); Escuela Nacional de Agricultura, *Información estadística de la población escolar: período 1966 a 1976* (Chapingo: Departamento de Planeación, 1976); and unpublished statistics, Departamento de Servicios Académicos, Colegio de Postgraduados, Chapingo, 1982.

[d]Interview material from 1981 and 1982. Professionals in fields which are not characterized by entrance examinations use various means to obtain employment in the public sector, which are discussed further in Chapter 4. Lawyers depend on recommendations via *camarillas* (reciprocal loyalty networks) throughout the public sector. Architects also are organized in loose *camarillas*, which compete among themselves for the major positions and contracts in SAHOP. School affiliation (*escuelismo*) plays a large role in the engineering fields, except in the Comisión Federal de Electricidad, where the union generally disallows management from applying examinations and clears all engineers for employment after the requisite payment.

agronomy. This system produces, on the one hand, a small number of competent professionals who obtain coveted positions and begin promising careers. On the other, it generates an extraordinary number of dropouts who have failed to achieve their initial goal. Unemployment among graduates of medical, legal, and economics programs, although difficult to measure, is high, and agronomy and petroleum engineering may follow suit.

This process is schematically represented in Fig. 1. The circle is completed when the unemployed and disenchanted coalesce to exert a social pressure that is felt by the state. This phenomenon has not yet occurred in Mexico, as it has in other countries, such as India.

STUDENT ENROLLMENT AND ACADEMIC DETERIORATION

Leading Mexican professionals are fully conversant with the pattern presented in Fig. 1. Those teaching in the universities feel that the major change over the past two decades has been in enrollment. The increased size of the student body has had repercussions on academic organization, teaching, learning, and professional practice. Between 1966 and 1979 the number of UNAM students and teachers increased by 430 percent, to 402,601.[8] In petroleum engineering, for example, the discoveries of oil and gas reservoirs sparked student interest in the field. From 1940 to 1980, UNAM graduated 674 petroleum engineers. In 1980, 843 undergraduate students were enrolled, 65 percent of them in the first two semesters.[9] The figures, however, remain small compared with those in agronomy, which in 1980 had nearly forty thousand students nationwide, and medicine, which enrolls about twenty-five thousand new students each year, despite growing unemployment in the field.

The increased student enrollment is correlated with a decline in academic quality, and apparently is furthered by the government's creation of new undergraduate programs in Mexico City and the provinces. Academic deterioration is most evident in teaching style and in light demands on students. Professors find that in a class of two hundred to three hundred students standard didactic methods are unworkable. The class becomes a crowd to which they direct their lectures. The students cannot ask questions, and the professors gain no sense of their personalities, capabilities, or even their objectives in taking the course. Teachers' motivation declines. Unable to take time for open discussion, they have no way to verify whether the students have understood their lectures. The students conclude that if teachers

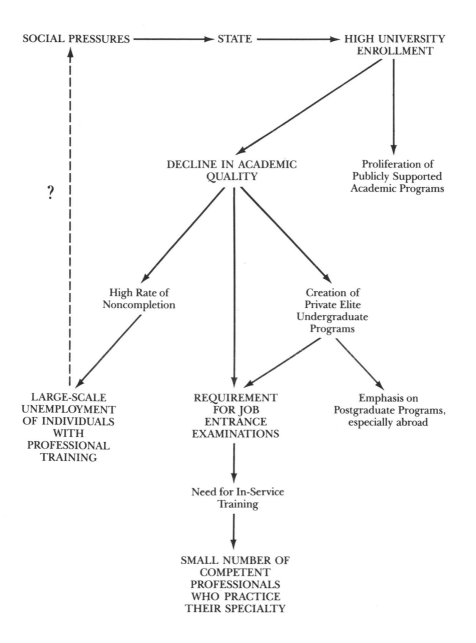

Figure 1. The State, Professional Training, and Unemployment

do not demand certain learning and analytical skills, no one will. They develop a passive attitude toward fulfilling their requirements and do not delve deeply into the subject matter. An experienced law professor described his impression:

> The students transform themselves into a cloudy mass of faces, to which the professor expounds 'bla, bla, bla.' The students simply listen. This goes on day after day . . . . The outcome is serious. The students, who are poorly prepared, eventually become judges. When the knowledgeable jurist confronts the politician in the courtroom, the judge favors the politician because the judge does not know the law well enough to appreciate the jurist's position.[10]

A parallel occurrence is that undergraduate teaching is permeated by leftist political organization, and considerable *grilla* (political intrigue) buffets the departments. Pressures are exerted on professors to lower requirements, and teachers and departmental heads who do not cooperate frequently are forced out.[11] Student preoccupation with international political issues, over which they exert little influence, distracts from academic pursuits.

The proliferation of undergraduate teaching programs has been most notable in agronomy, medicine, law, and economics, while UNAM and the Polytechnical Institute remain the key public institutions in petroleum engineering. Traditionally, the main schools of agronomy were Chapingo (Universidad Autónoma de Chapingo and Colegio de Postgraduados), Juárez (Escuela Superior Hermanos Escobar), Monterrey Tech (ITESM), and Saltillo (Universidad Autónoma Agraria Antonio Narro). During the Echeverría government, the state raised the number of schools to more than thirty at the undergraduate level, and 10 at the master's level.[12] In law, heavy student pressure to enter study programs in the provinces has derived less from youth's interest in jurisprudence than a desire for political careers. University authorities have felt they could launch such programs by appointing local judges and notary publics as part-time professors and opening the doors to student matriculation. In 1982 there were sixty-two degree-granting law programs in Mexico. Until 1910, Mexico had only nine medical schools; in 1979 there were forty-six, together with pressure on an increasing number of provincial universities to offer medical diplomas.[13] The dispersal of resources among newly created programs makes it difficult to maintain and improve the quality of existing programs. While the total state budget dedicated to professional education grows larger, fewer funds exist to pay for libraries, laboratories, classrooms, student research, and faculty salaries at specific institutions. Low salaries make an academic teaching career unattractive to the bright graduates who are well suited to transmit knowledge from one generation to the next. Talented faculty are lured away by government or private enterprise. Faculty/student ratios deteriorate. Professionals in teaching are exasperated by the situation. In the words of an economist:

> The economics professors (at my institution) have ridiculously low salaries. When we try to increase our budgets, it's as if we are asking personal favors. The budget discussions are traumatic and irrational.[14]

PRIVATE UNIVERSITIES AND POSTGRADUATE STUDIES

The decline in academic quality has led to (a) the creation of privately funded undergraduate university programs for those students who can afford them, (b) an increased emphasis on postgraduate training to qualify for professional employment, and (c) greater reliance by employers on strict entrance examinations to select the most competent professionals. These hurdles succeed in discouraging many students, who never complete their undergraduate programs or do not pass job qualifying examinations, and who add their numbers to the ranks of the professionally trained unemployed.

Private university programs have been most prominent in the field of economics, although important private professional schools also exist in medicine (Autonomous University of Guadalajara), agronomy (Monterrey Institute of Technology), and law (Iberoamerican University, a Catholic institution). The National School of Economics at UNAM was founded in the mid-1930s to train public functionaries with a broader vision than that of simple accountants or lawyers. Since the 1950s, and especially after ENE's swing to the left, economic and religious elites have founded private institutions which, lacking state subsidies, require comparatively expensive tuition and registration fees. Economics programs at ITESM (in Monterrey, home of the country's most dynamic industrialists), ITAM (the Autonomous Technological Institute of Mexico), Iberoamerican University, and Anáhuac University (the last three programs in Mexico City) offer a solid technical curriculum.

Partially because students pay for their education, academic standards are high. The graduates' overall better success in obtaining employment in the state sector, compared to ENE graduates, attracts enough students to allow the private universities to show operating profits.

Another means of filtering out aspirants for professional careers is to make postgraduate training a prerequisite, especially when it must be pursued in foreign countries. In the 1940s the Bank of Mexico sent young professionals abroad for economics training, and after 1945 foreign philanthropical foundations financed Mexican agronomists to attend United States graduate programs.[15] In 1959 the Colegio de Postgraduados was founded at Chapingo as the country's first master's degree program, and El Colegio de México began offering M.A. degrees in economics in 1965. The level of minimum training a student has needed to excel in agronomy and economics has been pushed upward, to the point that today's doctorate from a foreign university (or at least doctoral coursework completed) is a sine qua non for a promising career. A similar trend is emerging in petroleum engineering. Whereas few petroleum engineers from before 1940 have graduate degrees, most PEMEX and IMP staff born afterwards have earned an M.S. degree abroad. The situation is ambiguous in medicine. State medical institutes encourage doctors to specialize, but not abroad, because frequently they do not return. Only in law is postgraduate training immaterial for a successful public sector post, private practice, or a political career.

The public sector has recognized the value of postgraduate training abroad in the professions as a means of importing skills into Mexico. The response has been massive, rather than selective and quality-controlled, and resembles the policies that have resulted in large enrollments at the undergraduate level. The specter of large petroleum income encouraged the state to seek safety in numbers. CONACYT, the Science and Technology Council, planned to send 26,000 students abroad for graduate studies between 1976 and 1982.[16] If all these students were to return with degree in hand (data on completion rates are unavailable), the country would indeed enhance its collective professional and scientific competence. The principal criticism is that through such programs government resources flow to foreign institutions rather than improve the quality of undergraduate and graduate programs in Mexico. In the words of a skeptic:

> I visited U.S. universities and heard administrators tell me that they need foreign students to make up their operating deficits. We are sending hordes of people to Colorado, California, and Washington to solve their problems, not ours. I was told by a British professor that it was all right to offer substandard postgraduate training because all that foreign students needed was a piece of paper to become a secretary of state. This is immoral and we are willing dupes![17]

Postgraduate studies abroad are supported by benefitting students, who hope to compensate for poor training at the undergraduate level, and by the state, which is anxious to show that it is concerned about professional competence. In the last analysis, postgraduate training of any sort has the effect of prolonging the university career and of creating new hurdles for professional employment.

PROFESSIONAL CERTIFICATION BY EMPLOYERS

Employers are the de facto certifiers of professional competence in Mexico. The principal instrument is the job placement examination, administered by professionals at many large institutions that hire university graduates in significant numbers. The typical employer is faced with a crop of potential recruits who have a wide range of educational backgrounds and formal degrees, the quality of which cannot be accepted at face value. Through the examination process, the employer can test the applicants' knowledge and basic skills, despite the known pitfalls of standardized tests. The general pattern is that those who pass the tests have attended licenciate programs with high academic standards (which in many fields means at private universities) or graduate programs abroad, which require knowledge of a foreign language.[18]

In medicine, the pertinent examination admits doctors to residency in one of the public health institutions: IMSS, SSA, ISSSTE, PEMEX, and the DIF. Approximately fourteen-thousand take the exam each year; only a tenth pass it, and thus qualify for a three-year internship in a state hospital.[19] The remainder have the choice of starting an individual practice in a saturated urban area (or in a rural region suffering from a shortage of doctors), or joining the ranks of unemployed doctors and eventually seeking alternative employment. The dismal statistics on the doctor/population ratio in rural areas attest to the fact that few choose the countryside.[20] Most give up their plans for a medical career.

Public agencies employing lawyers, agronomists, economists, and petroleum engineers also use the qualifying examination as a means of selecting the most competent job seekers. The Bank of Mexico conducts entrance examinations every year, and finds that only a small percentage of those who pass are graduates of UNAM's ENE.[21] The National Institute of Agricultural Research holds two types of tests several times a year. Approximately 45 percent fail the technical examination, which leaves INIA short of manpower for its programs. It also gives a psychological test to ascertain adaptability to the organization's working style. Applicants who score well on the psychological test, having failed the technical test, often are brought into the institution and take special courses to strengthen their technical capabilities.[22] Even though PEMEX and IMP demand for petroleum engineers exceeds the available supply, they have given qualifying exams to prospective applicants with the intention of improving the skills of those who pass with a low grade. The Attorney General's offices of the Nation and of the Federal District, the Secretariat of Labor, and the Supreme Court also provide in-service courses for fully accredited lawyers so that their competence will meet minimal standards.

The remainder slip out of the system at one point or another. Of those who entered the university with a professional career in mind, some leave early in their studies for diverse reasons: marriage, economic insolvency, or lack of interest. Others (called *egresados* or *pasantes*) complete their formal coursework, but do not complete the licenciate thesis or other requirements for graduation and, therefore, do not graduate. Table 1 indicates that the ratio of graduates to *egresados* is low. Those who fail to pass the qualifying examinations for job placement usually join the ranks of unemployed professionals. Few opt for starting private practices, and most gradually shift into other occupations in which their training is immaterial.

During the 1970s petroleum engineers and agronomists had little difficulty locating gainful employment, but the situation was likely to change in the future as more graduates competed for a limited number of jobs. A seasoned veteran at Chapingo projected that

> the future of agronomy will be characterized by a large number of very bad agronomists. They will have to be content with lowly paid posts or those in routine administration. At the same time, you will have elites in the profession who are highly qualified, with extensive graduate training, who will dominate (prestige and power in) the profession.[23]

If the prediction proves accurate, agronomy would begin to resemble law and economics, and possibly be a projection of the trend in petroleum engineering.

THE EFFECTS OF NON-REGULATION

Unregulated by an official body, enrollment in university training programs in professional studies has reached mammoth proportions. The wide discrepancy between available employment and the size of the student body indicates that the state is unwilling or unable to balance supply with demand. The enrollment policies substantiate the view that professional training is not the primary purpose of university programs. Rather, the university is a means of providing temporary activity and prestige to young adults from poor socioeconomic backgrounds who, if they did not attend the university, would be marginally employed, if at all, and possibly engage in antisocial behavior or actions against the political system. Some students persevere to the point of earning a diploma, and a few actually achieve their initial goal of a professional career. These instances of a few successful candidates help transfer the burden of responsibility for failure of drop-outs to the drop-outs as individuals, thus defusing collective action on grievances. It is conceivable that in the future the political activity of unemployed professionals will represent a pressure on the state, and force fundamental changes in the current patterns.

The justification for lax admissions policies at publicly supported universities is that larger numbers of students from less wealthy backgrounds can enter the professions. The map of alternative routes to success is contorted, however, and in the last analysis the winners in the game of professional education have family backgrounds much different from the socioeconomic profile of the entering class at UNAM. Gainfully employed professionals usually are from privileged classes, which, according to political rhetoric, is one of the outcomes that mass professional education is supposed to avoid.

CHAPTER 4

The Organized Promotion of Professional Interests

Professionals aspire to advance their careers. Collective action often helps achieve this objective. Conventional wisdom says that the formal professional association, acting in the membership's interests, abets individual advancement. In Mexico, however, formal professional associations are not appropriate social organizations to protect the interests of the profession as a whole, and rarely have a direct effect on advancing individual careers. Instead of formal professional associations, other forms of organization have emerged in Mexico to respond to professionals' ambitions for employment, income and prestige.

In his work on professional associations, Geoffrey Millerson argues that the objectives of professional associations are to organize, qualify, promote study, register competence, and preserve high standards among professionals.[1] Secondary functions are to raise professional status, control entry into the professions, protect the profession and the public, act as an interest group, encourage social activity, and provide welfare benefits. He observes that they evolve into one or another type, and he focuses most attention on qualifying associations, which set up entrance requirements for individuals to practice a particular occupation.

Millerson's taxonomy is a useful starting point for dissecting professional associations in liberal capitalist societies, where an important objective has been to exclude the untrained and uninitiated from the marketplace.[2] Professional associations were

[59]

founded in Europe and the United States in part to counter charlatanry and fraud. Prior to the consolidation of professional associations, the marketplace was flooded with would-be doctors, surgeons, lawyers, and engineers. Membership in the association provided individuals with a standard "letter of credit" testifying to their worth. Consequently, the professional association could regulate the marketplace. The result was that fees for duly anointed professionals increased, especially as legislation made their services obligatory in certain transactions.

The professional associations also helped dampen individual entrepreneurship. Even with a reduced universe of certified professionals, their collective interests were not advanced when they competed furiously with one another for clients. Professional associations have stimulated specialization and decorum. Professionals were encouraged to focus on a limited part of their field and to stimulate business within it. The association encouraged professionals to settle their differences "in house," so as not to risk usurpation of self-regulation by the state or another official body, which would suppress the profession's autonomy. Professionals recognized the value of such discretion, and were loath to discredit fellow colleagues directly (for example, testifying against them in civil suits) or indirectly (such as advertising, which was often considered unethical).

In alliance with the university, the prototypical association established boundaries around the knowledge base of the profession and certified the acceptable techniques within it. Individuals or groups who used methodologies that fell outside these bounds were denounced as amateurs, even as dangerous amateurs. The association was organized to act quickly, often through legal channels, when such deviants threatened the profession's monopoly. Simultaneously, the professional association was responsible for updating its members' knowledge of new and acceptable ways of practicing the trade. Thus seminars, journals, and research were important parts of the association's activities.

A vibrant professional association provided multiple opportunities for professionals to interact. In this way professionals found friends, business partners, and young disciples. Associations were important to their members for social expression, networking, and employment. One's reputation was enhanced by the particular network of contacts maintained in the profession, and election to leadership posts in the association bestowed unquestioned prestige. For young professionals, dedication to the activities of the association was a time-tested means of improving employment opportunities and income.

In Britain and the United States, professional associations have limited their public policy interventions mainly to matters directly concerning the profession, such as certification and support for graduate education. This restraint is consistent with the precepts of liberal democratic theory. When each sub-group energetically pursues its own interests, and the political system balances interests over time, the theory holds that the good of society emerges. In fact, these associations are wary of the power of the state and are uninterested in incurring the wrath of government executives or legislators over matters that do not immediately affect their income and autonomy. If it were to meddle in tangential issues, the association fears that it might trigger a chain reaction. Offended parties would closely examine the body of myths by which the profession justifies itself, and find them to be wanting. By limiting its lobbying to matters of immediate concern, the profession avoids risk, strengthens its claim of "professionalism," and retains its maximum influence for consequential issues, which usually involve keeping the state out of the business its members control and avoiding competition from outsiders.

These statements refer to ideal professional associations in liberal capitalist societies. At least three caveats are in order. First, professional associations rarely are fully integrated and participative.[3] Leadership tends to be oligarchic. Only a small number of professionals sustains the organization at the center, and the periphery is passive. The rank and file join mainly for certification, or to be "in good standing." Second, licensing and self-regulation frequently do little to protect the public, since professionals are loath to criticize or correct their colleagues:

> "Whether it be medicine, law, or any other privileged work group, ephemeral criteria and claims to special expertise, in-group solidarity and secrecy, and the lack of active or powerful regulatory bodies all combine to make professional peer control honored more in the breach than in the observance."[4]

Third, although some Mexican professional associations aspire to liberal ideals, Mexico is not a liberal capitalist country and professional associations should not be scaled according to an inappropriate standard.

Previous chapters suggested some of the differences between the evolution of professions in Mexico and in other societies. The Mexican state is more powerful and dominant over professions. Schooling does not, in and of itself, restrict access to the professions; indeed, an open admissions policy floods the professions. None of the professions treated in this study is predominantly liberal, in the sense that the typical professional interacts mainly with individual clients; government agencies provide the major source of employment, even for doctors.

The literature gives short shrift to professional organization in centralist, corporatist, or Third World countries in general. In the Soviet Union, independently constituted professional associations are uncommon, and neither lawyers nor economists have national professional associations.[5] Writers are an exception, but the Writers' Union's "functions and freedom of expression are directly or indirectly controlled by the state or, more properly speaking, by the Communist Party."[6] Most professionals express their interests through their scientific academy or place of employment. Their professional interests are reduced to labor matters, or are coterminus with the orientation of the bureaucratic unit. Professional associations in corporatist-like systems have not been researched. Extrapolating from theories of corporatism, an analyst would expect that professional groups would be nonconflictive, community-oriented, all-inclusive (i.e., require membership from all licensed professionals), and beholden to the state for orientation.[7]

Mexican professional organizations do not fall neatly into any of these categories, although each model suggests features found in one or another professional grouping. The protective instinct among professionals, however, exists in Mexico as elsewhere.[8] The difference is that, to further their individual and collective goals, Mexican professionals either resort to other organizational forms, or mold the formal features of professional associations in ways appropriate to the Mexican system. The most important groups are those linked to political parties, networks of individuals who share reciprocal loyalties, university alumni associations, labor unions, and interest groups within state agencies. Each profession in Mexico is characterized predominantly by one or another of these forms, but not all are equally effective. All coexist with formal professional associations, whose vitality and scope of activity differ according to historical conditions affecting the evolution of each profession.

In general, the peak professional associations in each field offer opportunities for social expression, some prestige for the individuals elected to leadership posts, a journal (not heavily subscribed), and sponsor occasional seminars or meetings. They do not define the core of knowledge in the field, regulate entry, dampen individual entrepreneurship, or facilitate employment. These functions either are ignored or are carried out by other organizational structures. Some of these other forms have proven their worth and thus professionals have found them to be attractive. They can be employment networks and income guarantors. They also have helped locate professionals in top state posts, and on occasion influence public policy in their fields.

Most professionals consider the activities of their formal associations trivial. Aspiring professional leaders often find it advantageous to link up with the dominant political party or to restrict their organizing activities to the period around presidential elections. Groups of reciprocal loyalties (*camarillas*) are most predominant among lawyers, alumni associations among agronomists, professional unions within state agencies among doctors, and a trade union joining both professionals and workers among petroleum engineers. Economists appear to have constituted a nationally based professional association, which encompasses and transcends many of the particularistic elements of the above structures. The National College of Economists is an ambitious body attempting to carry out professional functions under the constraints posed by the Mexican political system.

FORMAL PROFESSIONAL ASSOCIATIONS

The Law of Professions dictates that each profession must have at least one professional association with the following objectives: encourage graduates to register their degrees, draw up a list of practicing professionals, propose fees and honoraria, collaborate with universities in planning course curricula, arbitrate professional conflicts, denounce violations of the law, sanction members who do not abide by professional standards, and consult with government on matters of mutual concern. The law additionally provides that the General Agency of Professions can register up to five associations in the Federal District and up to five in each state.[9]

The oldest continuous professional association that now qualifies as one of the national "colleges" is the Illustrious and National College of Lawyers, whose origins extend back to 1760. Other such colleges and their founding dates are: National Academy of Medicine (1864), the College of Architects (1945), the College of Engineers (1946), the National College of Agronomic Engineers (1947), the National College of Economists (1952), and the National College of Petroleum Engineers (1973).[10] Table 2 offers information on major professional associations in Mexico, including those linked to the official party PRI.[11]

The general opinion of professionals is that these associations are ineffective. The National Academy is one of the few officially recognized professional associations for which membership is by invitation only. Similar to Millerson's prestige association, it consists of a select group of doctors with incontrovertible talent and medical experience. But its influence is limited; even those

Table 2 Professional Associations in Mexico, 1982

Professional Field	Name of Principal College Date of Founding Membership (approx) Journal Title Paid Subscriptions (approx)	Names of Other Associations Officially Registered in the Federal District	Names of Professional Associations Affiliated with the PRI
Law	Ilustre y Nacional Colegio de Abogados 1760 204 *Contemporánea* (last issue 1976) 2,000	Barra Mexicana Asociación Nacional de Abogados Colegio del Sindicato de Abogados del Distrito Federal Colegio de Abogados "Foro de México" Federación Nacional de Colegios de Abogados	Abogados Revolucionarios de México Federación de Abogados Mexicanos Asociación Nacional de Abogados "Belisario Domínguez"
Medicine	Academia Nacional de Medicina 1864 340 *Gaceta Médica de México* (monthly) 5,000	Colegio Nacional de Médicos Cirujanos "Dr. Eduardo Liceaga" Colegio de Cirujanos Colegio de Médicos "Post-Graduados del Hospital General del Centro Médico Nacional del IMSS" Federación Nacional de Colegios de la Profesión Médica	Agrupación Política de Médicos Mexicanos Asociación Nacional de Médicos Revolucionarios Congreso de la Medicina
Architecture	Colegio de Arquitectos de México 1945 2,700 *Arquitectura y Sociedad* (monthly) 8,500	Colegio Nacional de Ingenieros Arquitectos Colegio de Maestros en Arquitectura, Restauradores de Sitios y Monumentos Federación de Colegios de Arquitectos de la República Mexicana	Agrupación de Arquitectos Revolucionarios Agrupación Femenina de Arquitectos

Civil Engineering	Colegio de Ingenieros Civiles 1946 5,900 *Ingeniería Civil* (bi-monthly) 6,000	None	Sociedad Mexicana de Ingenieros Vanguardia de Arquitectos e Ingenieros Asociación de Ingenieros Industriales, Mecánicos, Electricistas, y Químicos del Estado de Michoacán
Agronomy	Colegio de Ingenieros Agrónomos 1947 2,000 *Ingeniería Agronómica* (monthly) Unavailable	None	Confederación Nacional de Organizaciones Agronómicas Asociación Mexicana de Profesionistas Forestales
Economics	Colegio Nacional de Economistas 1952 3,000 *El Economista Mexicano* (bi-monthly) 3,000	None	Federación Mexicana de Mujeres Economistas Asociación Mexicana de Economistas al Servicio del Estado Asociación Mexicana de Profesionales de la Economía Frente de Economistas Mexicanos Economía y Comercio Exterior Liga de Economistas Revolucionarios de la República Federación Nacional de Mujeres Economistas
Petroleum Engineering	Colegio de Ingenieros Petroleros 1973 1,200 *Boletín Informativo* 1,200	Colegio de Ingenieros de Minas, Metalurgistas, Petroleros y Geólogos de México Asociación de Ingenieros Petroleros	None

Sources: Column 1: information provided by the respective professional associations; column 2: Dirección General de Profesiones; column 3: Comité Ejecutivo Nacional, Confederación Nacional de Organizaciones Populares, Partido Revolucionario Institucional.

doctors who belong do not consider it to be their representative medical association. The consensus among leaders of the profession is that medicine is not a professional guild in Mexico, and the Academy is not a corporation of interests. Assisting government is one of the Academy's main functions, and it is capable of forming study groups in almost all specialties, including veterinary medicine and sanitary engineering. However, the examples of public functionaries consulting the Academy on its opinion concerning public health matters or the organization of health services in Mexico are few. The Academy dedicates much of its attention to promoting medical specialties in Mexico.

Similar patterns prevail in other formal professional associations. The College of Agronomic Engineers was created subsequent to the December 23, 1944, law requiring each profession to have an official body. All those who have their degrees registered with the General Agency of Professions are eligible to apply for membership. In principle, the College does not pursue political ends and is empowered to carry out formal activities to strengthen the profession. Few agronomists feel that the College has effectively disseminated professional values, improved competence, or helped set national priorities.[12]

With respect to the Illustrious and National College of Lawyers, a young up-and-coming lawyer, who already had achieved a senior position in the para-state sector, commented:

> There is a lack of interest among lawyers in the professional associations. No one cares about the College of Lawyers. Why is this so? No one has time to go to meetings.[13]

A university-based lawyer elaborates:

> There are many supposed representative organs for the law profession. None has the moral authority to represent what lawyers have studied. There may be fifty of these units which claim that they represent all lawyers, and the Illustrious and National College is just one of them . . . . We three persons in this room could start a bar association, but it wouldn't mean anything.[14]

Of those surveyed, associations dealing with petroleum engineering appear to coincide most closely with the model envisioned by the legal code and statutes. The role of the College of Petroleum Engineers is to serve as a consulting group to the state-owned industry on oil development, and to promote greater knowledge in the field. The College organizes seminars and meetings, encourages professional training, provides speakers on petroleum policy for civic groups, and issues publicity on university programs. A parallel organization is the Association of Petroleum Engineers, founded in 1959, whose open membership includes chemical and mechanical engineers, PEMEX employees, and representatives of private companies supplying the petroleum industry. Professedly nonpolitical, its attractions include friendship, professional interaction and conferences, a journal, and a mutual fund life insurance program. Speeches at monthly meetings treat themes of current interest, and the yearly congress, attended by members and nonmembers, awards prizes for the best scholarly papers. The Association permits the membership to interact with a number of institutions and individuals involved in the petroleum field. Partaking of Association activities, more so than in those of the College, has been helpful in advancing the careers of young engineers within PEMEX.

The popularity of the associations in petroleum engineering is explained in part by professional dissatisfaction with the major organization in the field, namely, the omnibus union in PEMEX to which virtually all engineers must belong. Abuses and corruption in the union apparently have induced petroleum engineers to seek shelter in the associations, whose members share common values and class extraction. The PEMEX union is considered later in this chapter.

In general, however, most professionals consider their formal associations immaterial for protecting and advancing their interests.

POLITICAL POSTS

Ambitious individuals in the formally constituted professional association frequently try to occupy association leadership posts in order to gain visibility among political authorities, and often organize groups of professionals to support the presidential candidates of the PRI. In these cases, formal functions of the professional association are displaced through efforts to curry favor within the political system. In the first case, professionals with political ambitions take the necessary steps to be "elected" head of one or another "representative" professional group so that they can legitimately request a hearing before public authorities and possibly elevate themselves as prime candidates for bureaucratic posts. In the second case, professionals appeal to the politicians' need for legitimation in a one-party political system. Politicians are eager to have the backing of professionals whose wise political judgment presumably matches their technical skill. If the professionals have gone out on a limb and made public their support of a candidate who has not yet been ratified, the rewards in political and bureaucratic posts are likely to be much greater should that person emerge victorious. These patterns have been most prevalent recently in agronomy, accounting, and law.

The Confederación de Organizaciones Agronómicas is the association in agronomy affiliated with the PRI. Founded in 1922 as the Mexican Agronomic Society, it is considered part of the National Peasants' Confederation (CNC), one of the three pillars of the PRI (the others being workers and the "popular" sector). Agronomists are automatically incorporated into the Confederation, irrespective of whether they have their licenciate degrees. Traditionally, it has supported the agrarian reform, but its political views are ambiguous, depending on the political winds of the time. The head of the Confederation makes a point of pledging his allegiance to the current and future presidents of the country.

Agronomists obtain high posts in government by maximizing their personal and professional assets in ways valued by the political system. They cultivate a reputation for efficiency and trustworthiness with the Secretary of Agriculture, other secretaries, the future president, and the current president. Although short-term changes can occur within the same *sexenio*, or six-year presidential term, most agronomists have a long-term perspective. They want to know where they will be when jobs are distributed in the next *sexenio*. They come to judgments on the identity of the future president, and on the agronomist whom the future president probably will consult for the top positions in the agricultural agencies.

Before the presidential election, the Confederation of Agronomic Organizations (the PRI appendage) and the College of Agronomic Engineers are elevated in importance. When high-level political aspirants begin to gather around each potential PRI candidate, they need to establish relations with agronomists. Since they do not necessarily know the names of the most competent agronomists, they consult with the professional associations. The director of one of these associations has a priceless opportunity to mold his own future, and possibly to become the leading agronomist for one of these groups. If he is lucky, everything ends well. But since there are many precandidates, demonstrable loyalty to one can be risky. Under Echeverría, López Portillo was a dark horse, and no group formed around him. Agronomists lined up behind other candidates. Upon his selection, López Portillo consciously avoided appointing agronomists to work with him who had been active supporters of one of his adversaries. Agronomists learned their lesson and were much more circumspect in manifesting political preferences until López Portillo's own successor was announced.[15]

In the pre-electoral period, professional associations spring to life, and internal elections are of utmost importance. The professional leader, if he plays his cards correctly, is in an excellent position to move to a top government post. Sometimes transitory organizations emerge. In the months preceding the *destape* (unveiling) of the PRI candidate for the 1982 election, the Subsecretary of Planning and Budgeting, Ramón Aguirre Velázquez, a public accountant, founded an association of "accountants in the service of the state." Nominally 10,000 strong, its main purpose was to declare support for Miguel de la Madrid's candidacy for the PRI's nomination. The move was a cause célèbre because it preceded the *destape* by six months. Aguirre Velázquez was criticized from practically every corner except de la Madrid's camp, because he had violated President López Portillo's request that electoral maneuvering be kept unobtrusive. Furthermore, his political sophistication was faulted because he was placing his own future in jeopardy should de la Madrid be passed over. In fact, de la Madrid was selected as the PRI candidate and Aguirre's future cabinet position was assured. Reflecting on the accountants' affair, an informant quipped, "In the same way, around election time, you have the associations of chewing-gum vendors and druggists who produce a letterhead which will last only as long as the campaign."[16] Virtually all constituencies want to be on the good side of the winning candidate.

Competition for leadership positions in the recognized associations can be fierce in the pre-election period. One lawyer described the proceedings as follows:

> The bar association has an election via a methodology we have perfected. The election is announced a day after it has taken place. Phantom names have voted for preselected candidates. The opposing lawyers protest, even occupying buildings. Can you imagine this from lawyers? What do you expect of the system of justice when they behave like this?[17]

These practices, although common, are by nature transitory, since they occur in the months preceding presidential elections. Most professionals have more permanent structures and networks to protect and further their interests, but these are separate from formal professional associations.

RECIPROCAL LOYALTY NETWORKS

Mutual reciprocity networks exist in Mexico, as in other countries. In Mexico, those with the widest scope commonly are called *camarillas*, and are populated mainly by lawyers.[18] A small number of lawyers in the bureaucracy, those who make their careers within a juridical speciality (such as criminal law, labor law, or habeas corpus), follow career paths that do not require membership in a *camarilla*. Moreover, the predominant organizational forms for other professions have more restricted boundaries, based on school affiliation (agronomy), union affiliation (petroleum engineering), and ministerial partitions (medicine, economics). Doctors and petroleum engineers generally do not recognize that their professions are integrated into national *camarillas*; agronomists feel these links have declined considerably since the 1950s, and economists claim that personal loyalties are less important than divisions in schools of economic thought.

Most lawyers in the public sector are administrators and aspirants to top-level political posts. Their training in law is incidental to their duties in the bureaucracy, and they must pay close attention to their network of political relations. As students, soon after entering the university, they try to use their existing contacts, such as a relative or a professor, to obtain a part-time job in the public sector. By broadening their circle of friends at university and on the job, they subsequently seek promotions in the bureaucracy. The lack of a career ladder makes membership in a *camarilla* essential. A change in the head of the ministry means that all upper-level and many lower-level jobs are vacated in favor of the new appointee's supporters and friends. The prevailing belief among lawyers is that they need to pursue their careers through personal relations, and are never appointed or promoted because of merit.

An interview with a female lawyer contained comments illustrating this pattern. She explained that

> the group phenomenon is quite prominent in the law profession. You might call them 'tiny mafias,' but that is not an adequate term. There is no great consensus among lawyers but many groups, such as Alemán's. These groups, moreover, can be friendly toward each other, and they are not necessarily organized along ideological lines. You don't find groups of lawyers identified with points of view strictly to the Left or to the Right. When people are clearly marked ideologically, they run a risk.[19]

On pursuing one's career:

> A career is made through political dealings. One has to have many contacts and relations. The person who gets ahead is not necessarily more capable, professionally speaking. He does not have to have better academic preparation. One is subjected to the ups and downs of political change. Career-making is very difficult for all professions, especially lawyers. If a director is forced to fire either a

lawyer or an engineer, he will fire the lawyer. The engineer knows things that can be valuable in the public sector.

On sexual biases:

Being a woman makes it three times more difficult, like in all parts of Mexican society. There is a high degree of sexual discrimination. Perhaps only Iran and the Arab countries are more discriminatory than Mexico. The cases of women who have made a successful career in the public sector are exceptional. They have had to accumulate experience and political management skills far beyond those required of a man. Here feminism is a question of quotas to portray a democratic image. In the Chamber of Deputies, there is always a quota of women. It doesn't make any difference to which political party they belong. Likewise, it is customary for one woman to fill a high-ranking administrative post. We joke that these women are like token Negroes in U.S. films. To succeed in the bureaucracy, it is a terrible ideological and sexual struggle.[20]

Under the circumstances, a *camarilla* is vital:

A lawyer needs to be a member of a group and be faithful to that group. The lawyer can't leave doors or options open to chance. If you are very good and bright, you nonetheless need the protection from group contact. You have to learn political skills. You have to know many people so that you can feel secure that, no matter who is appointed above you, you can always call a friend to retain your job. Within this political family, you are usually safe. Remember that the political class is economically powerful. A leading politician has no problem whatsoever staying outside the system during one presidential administration. It's not just anybody who can be six years without work and still survive. And we are not talking just of passing the time, but giving lavish presents and continuous entertainment. These people have the money to represent themselves, and can help out their supporters for long periods. The motto in Mexican political circles is just wait until your turn comes up again.

This lawyer concluded her summary of *camarillas* with the comment that these trends were not the same for other professions. The statement is, essentially, accurate. Most economists reject the idea that an integrated system of group or personal loyalties extends from them to an influential politician. Nor does the system predominate in PEMEX or the IMP, where only exceptionally does an engineer obtain an upper-middle-level post or below because of demonstrated loyalty to a politician. *Camarilla* affiliation apparently has declined in agronomy:

Groups of agronomists used to move in and out of public sector jobs as a bloc, but that is no longer the case today. The reason is that there is a high demand for agronomists. Everyone get his *chamba* (job) and is content. There is no need to join *camarillas*, and there aren't any, except maybe for an occasional one.[21]

Lawyers are ambitious for political and administrative office. They rely on *camarillas* more than do other professionals because *camarillas* are an effective way for them to exert oligopolistic control over the marketplace. Lawyers are not unionized or ideologically differentiated, and their skills are not essential to many parts of the state apparatus they would like to manage. Aside from their native intelligence, they have few opportunities to establish individual identities and thus distinguish themselves from competitors. By rallying around an influential leader, group members can concentrate their personal and professional resources to pursue their collective and individual interests. The system perseveres in part because, through their access to the main levers of public power, lawyers can be kind to themselves. The vanquished are not eliminated, but are sustained in one or another corner of the multifarious system to await their chance to return. While the winners' stakes are high, the prospect of defeat is not traumatic, and strong inducements for containing resentment help mitigate overt conflict.

That other professionals are less integrated into *camarillas* relates more to their relative political inefficacy than to any intrinsic features of their disciplines. *Camarillas* are not dominant cleavages in nonlegal professions because these professions at present are less politicized, and, unlike law, are not mobilized on a permanent basis to seek political power. Mexicans who seek high-level political appointments, irrespective of their field, need to incorporate themselves into a personal trust network. Professionals appointed to high positions because of their technical reputation need to begin demonstrating loyalty to the group that hired them and, in order to carry out their jobs successfully, to recruit other reliable persons for lower-level positions. When they do so, they are extending the range of the *camarilla* to which they implicitly belong. To the degree that other professional groups become more involved in political competition, they will act through existing or new *camarilla* networks.

SCHOOL LOYALTY

An agronomist differentiates among colleagues in the field on the basis of the school they attended. This phenomenon is called *escuelismo,* and is based on the fact that Mexico boasts several undergraduate schools of agronomy with established reputations, including Chapingo, Juárez, Monterrey Tech, and Saltillo. By contrast, petroleum engineering is taught in but two major schools (UNAM and the National Polytechnical Institute), and UNAM is the principal training ground for doctors and lawyers. While a number of quality schools exists in economics, economists tend to divide themselves according to those who attended the National Economics School (UNAM), the private undergraduate universities, or graduate school abroad, and by country of foreign study. The divisions are so numerous and each combination contains so few members that *escuelismo* in economics is diluted.

Multipurpose alumni associations are the organizational manifestation of *escuelismo* in agronomy. On the surface they appear to be highly informal. Elections are haphazard, and sometimes the president simply is reconfirmed without a ballot. Although organized into local chapters, there is no list of members and even nongraduates can attend meetings, which are held approximately once a month. The gatherings might include a speech, but they are primarily social and culminate in the enthusiastic singing of the school song. These associations' social activities, however, solidify membership participation for more weighty concerns, especially employment. The associations' political influence is expressed through their leaders (not necessarily the nominal head of the alumni group), who are veteran high-level functionaries known to leading politicians. Often these leaders maneuver to obtain elective positions in the Confederation of Agronomic Organizations or the College of Agronomic Engineers.

Most agronomists can refer to a half-dozen patriarchs who wield influence in the profession. While some can be identified as *campesinistas* (see Chapter 2), agricultural modernizers, or political compromisers, their ideological preferences usually are difficult to ascertain. They are more closely associated with the school from which they come and whose graduates they promote. In the 1980s, leading figures from Chapingo were Sergio Reyes Osorio, Eduardo Alvarez Luna, José Guevara Calderón, and José Rodríguez Vallejo; from Antonio Narro (Saltillo) came José Silos and Lorenzo Martínez; from Monterrey Tech came Jesús Moncada de la Fuente and Ricardo García; and from Juárez came José Díaz de León and Jaime Arteaga.

Agronomists from each school often try to place their people in good posts, and *escuelismo* describes the behavior of a new appointee to a public sector position who fills lower posts with alumni from his school. Competition over high-ranking jobs in agronomy and the lack of career structure perpetuate the system. One informant described the rate of mobility within the public sector as "frightening."[22] The alumni associations respond to this uncertainty, but with limited objectives. The alumni associations are not trying to enlarge the number of positions covered by agronomy. Rather, they attempt to place certain people in certain jobs. Typically, when someone interviews for a position either in the public or private sector, the first question is "Where did you go to school?" The answer is given, and the rest of the interview is colored by that piece of information. Chapingo's alumni association continues to be the most influential because of the school's age, outstanding professors, the sheer number of its students, and the widespread presence of its graduates in top-level public posts.

Many agronomists want *escuelismo* to disappear and less ascriptive criteria to emerge to establish professional credentials. They feel that *escuelismo* is a symptom of cultural underdevelopment, and cannot encompass the large number of new schools that have emerged in the agronomic field. Public agencies try to combat the trend by purposefully mixing graduates from different schools in the same work teams. To date, *escuelismo* has been relatively effective in achieving the goals of agronomic groups. Agronomists have not had to deal with the challenges of employment or promotion in the public sector as individuals, but have depended on broad networks of contacts, which are more specific than the *camarilla* and less universal than the formal professional association. If outside pressures force a change, another organizational form would need to come to the fore. For the moment, none appears to be on the horizon. Indeed, the multiplicity of agronomic schools is likely to reinforce the system, as graduates of traditional schools strive to maintain their hold over public service jobs.

UNIONIZATION OF DOCTORS

In the mid-1960s, sectors of the medical profession made an earnest but unsuccessful effort to devise a formula to defend collective interests. A strike spontaneously organized by interns and residents for better pay and working conditions nearly galvanized all public sector doctors into a single unit. The government succeeded in breaking the union, and memories of the event weigh heavily on those doctors who participated. Later, in the early 1970s, some petroleum engineers agitated for the creation of a union in PEMEX to monitor pay, promotions, and working conditions. After lengthy discussions, the PEMEX engineers were inducted by government fiat into the PEMEX workers' union. Unionization has had a negative effect on the esprit de corps of petroleum engineers. In neither case did unionization succeed in protecting the autonomy or interests of the professions. Doctors have responded by creating grievance committees organized by public sector agencies (IMSS, DIF, SSA, etc.), and petroleum engineers by participating more actively in their formally constituted professional associations. This section treats the doctors.

The 1965 strike movement originated in hospitals under the jurisdiction of the Secretaría de Salubridad y Asistencia.[23] The interns and residents wanted improved salaries, houses, training, libraries, and treatment facilities. The grievances had begun under the Adolfo López Mateos government, which in 1961 had refused to recognize a national union called the Asociación Médica Nacional. Matters came to a head under President Díaz Ordaz. The Alianza de Médicos Mexicanos, A.C., was registered in January 1965, after the government failed to take account of work-related complaints of AMMRIAC (Asociación Mexicana de Médicos Residentes e Internos, A.C.). The Alianza was made up of six thousand interns, who earned only 400 pesos per month (equivalent to US$16) their first year and 500 pesos the second year. The public sector treated salary for interns as a symbolic gratuity rather than a livelihood. After the youngest doctors started the movement, residents and almost all senior doctors joined in, and the strike spread to the rest of the public sector health services. The strikers succeeded in slowing down medical service until only one IMSS hospital was providing medical attention in Mexico City. The government stalled for time, knowing that many members of the profession were participating reluctantly in collective action.

The first strike lasted from April 20 to June 4, 1965. The Díaz Ordaz government at first denounced the movement, and then offered to negotiate the demands for better pay and obligatory membership in the union. The doctors returned to work. Dissatisfied with progress on meeting the demands, the Alianza leaders called another strike, which lasted from August 30 to September 7. The government increased pay to between Mex $1,500 and Mex $3,500 per month, and ordered doctors back to work. Simultaneously, most of the strike leaders were fired and several were jailed. One doctor described the government's reaction "as the most severe garrot seen in Mexico since the Porfiriato."[24] This exaggeration testifies to the impact the government's reaction had on doctors' nascent aspirations for self-regulation.

The movement raised the political consciousness of the medical profession, but the Alianza did not consolidate into a permanent professional union. One explanation relates to the individualistic nature of the profession. The doctor reputedly has to have a one-on-one relationship with the patient so as not to confuse one with another. Their atomized, or "feudal," orientation makes doctors hesitant to join organizations. The argument, however, fails to account for the success doctors in liberal capitalist societies have had in forming effective interest groups.

A more convincing explanation is that the Mexican state undermined the union by persecuting its leaders because authorities felt more comfortable keeping doctors in a bureaucratic relationship with the state in each public sector health institute.[25] Since then, maintenance of the status quo has been in the interests of the state and convenient for doctors. Politicians recognize that doctors, with their special skills and influence with patients, could be a formidable force. An organization of doctors with a clear corporate consciousness and the potential of developing independent political positions would threaten state control. Medical folk history reports that President Miguel Alemán in the 1940s saw fit to smother an organizing effort sponsored by the state. When approached with the idea of integrating them into the PRI, he said, "You want to organize doctors? Are you crazy?"[26]

A side effect of the 1965 strike was to direct doctors' organizational efforts to the workplace. The movement forced recognition of the rights of residents and interns in the state hospitals, and improved their working conditions, salaries, and instruction. Over time, the vertical separation of agencies employing doctors in the public sector and concern with work-related grievances have been a structural impediment to a nationwide doctors' movement. The public sector medical institutions are divided into distinct budgets and programs, with little joint planning or communication among doctors at operational levels. On occasion the National Academy urges that the medical system be unified, in order to provide comparable medical service throughout the country.[27] The suggestion is opposed by privileged beneficiaries of elite medicine (in PEMEX and ISSSTE), and by those who profit from the prevailing disarray. The divisions provide an opportunity for doctors to hold more than one job in the public sector. Reputable doctors consider *chambismo* to be an unethical characteristic of Mexican medicine; it formally is not permitted, but is not denounced openly because of professional courtesy. Under *chambismo*, a doctor might work in the IMSS for eight hours, and take his two hours at lunch in the ISSSTE. He shows up late in the afternoon for the IMSS, but records are not kept. Furthermore, he might work the night shift in the Federal District government and hold teaching posts at UNAM and the National Polytechnic Institute, for a total of five public sector jobs. Doctors engaging in *chambismo* are not interested in the unification of the health system because they would be unable to draw full salaries from their multiple places of employment. These doctors are the allies of officials who argue against unification for fear of creating favorable conditions for a nationwide doctors' movement.[28]

In the absence of a better alternative, doctors have emphasized medical specialization as a means of differentiating skills and prestige. They have also joined limited professional groupings that have formed in the state agencies, with membership drawn only from those doctors working in the institution. The most important grievance committees are the Association of Doctors in the IMSS and its counterparts in the Institutes of Cardiology and Tropical Diseases and the SSA hospitals and clinics. Doctors are capable of exerting some pressure within their institutions of employment, but only for such matters as compensation, fringe benefits, and labor conditions. As public employees, doctors still consider themselves poorly paid. Nor do they believe they have integrated professional criteria into state ideology in the public health sector.

Doctors face a paradoxical situation. The medical profession lacks effective organization, but it is able to extract a measure of protection from the political system. The doctors' power is latent, given the possibility of new work stoppages. Their aspirations for autonomy are dampened by obstacles in communicating with like-minded professionals in other public health agencies, and by painful recollections of 1965. The government tolerates their escape for half the workday to private practices or alternative employment. Furthermore, the government shelters their status by holding at bay the thousands of unemployed medical graduates who would willingly fill their jobs should state-employed doctors become obstreperous. Doctors are more oriented toward ideals of liberalism than are other professions in Mexico. Yet their dominant forms of organization are reminiscent of professions under a centralist system. Most doctors are conscious of their predicament, and many become cynical when discussing it. Professional leaders have few ideas on how to strengthen professional unity without risking their jobs or tarnishing their prestige. For the present, they sense that they are stalemated.

UNIONIZATION OF PETROLEUM ENGINEERS

Unionization of petroleum engineers has resulted in enhanced job protection and in more relaxed working conditions. Leaders in the field complain, however, that it has lowered morale, weakened authority, implicated professionals in the corruption that plagues the industry, and substituted false criteria for promotion.

After expropriation of the foreign oil companies, all workers, with the sole exception of PEMEX's general director, were included in the union.[29] In 1940 a consensus was reached that the arrangement was inefficient, and a new job category was created: *empleados de confianza*. These non-unionized "trusted employees" were paid salaries, not hourly wages, and were professionals at the complete disposal of the company, which could order them to leave for a well at any time of day or night. In the petroleum industry, emergencies were frequent and the company tended to take advantage of the engineers' commitment to their jobs. To be a petroleum engineer at the time, the young professional had to be hardy and ascetic. Logistical support, such as small planes, helicopters, lodging for the family, or air conditioning, was unknown. In the early days of nationalistic fervor, however, practically no one thought of forming a union. Problems between the engineers and management, such as petitions for higher pay, were resolved amicably. Strikes or work stoppages never entered the engineers' minds.

Petróleos Mexicanos grew from a total of 17,600 employees in 1938 to 36,500 workers in drilling and exploration alone in 1970 (71,000 overall).[30] The family atmosphere disappeared. Because of the demand for professionals, many *pasantes* were brought into the company. *Pasantes* were individuals who had taken all coursework for the engineering degree, but who had not completed the licenciate thesis needed to obtain the diploma. Despite receiving official encouragement and incentives from the company, many *pasantes* never finished the thesis, were skipped over for promotions, and tended to be relegated to outlying inhospitable terrain. As they became older they married, and the hardship was passed on to their families. Pasantes could not enter the Engineer A category, but had to remain technical assistants. Their pay was lower, and they believed that Petróleos Mexicanos discriminated against them. As they gained practical experience, their attitude was, "I know just as much as this other engineer who has his degree, so why should I earn less?"

The union movement was not a continuous process. Complaints were voiced in 1969 and 1970, and PEMEX reacted by dismissing the technicians who tried to organize engineers in the Gulf Coast city of Coatzacoálcos. The remainder of the engineers believed this step unjust, and prevailed on the company to reinstate them. No union was formed. In 1975, dissatisfied engineers renewed their efforts to form a separate union of professionals. Petróleos Mexicanos opposed the idea, as did a large segment of the engineers, who felt that professionals should not belong to unions. For them, the mark of a professional was relative continuity between working and nonworking hours.

Nonetheless, if a union was to be formed, the petroleum engineers wanted it to encompass only those with professional training. The government rejected that option because it did not want to have to negotiate with both a workers' union and a professional union.

After lengthy discussions and meetings, but with no vote on the engineers' preference, the government issued a decree that all engineers in PEMEX must belong to the Sindicato de Trabajadores Petroleros de la República Mexicana. One senior engineer, whose views represent those of the most experienced professionals, described March 18, 1976, as "the saddest day in the history of petroleum engineering" in Mexico. He continued with his opinion of the events: "Those who wanted to introduce the union were the bad elements in PEMEX. It is true that we were working too hard prior to unionization, sometimes twenty-four hours straight with no extra pay . . . We were exploited and our superiors did not understand. If they had, PEMEX would not have suffered work stoppages and strikes" and the union idea would not have emerged.[31]

Most petroleum engineers believe that unionization has been bad for Petróleos Mexicanos. First, the profession lost a measure of mystique. Petroleum engineers began to act like union workers, continuously watching the clock and keeping track of their benefits. Productivity declined. Previously, the engineers on set salary had to go to wells on Saturday and Sunday as a matter of course. Under union clauses, they were paid overtime, which increased costs to the company. While justified in the case of conscientious engineers, the clause led to widespread overtime claims to increase salary. Many engineers failed to accomplish what they should during working hours, and then used overtime to earn extra money. Unionization changed the mentality of many engineers, who felt they were, or should behave like, wage laborers.

Second, the union upset lines of authority and supervision in the company. Two interviewees provided examples on the basis of personal experience. A hardworking engineer in a pump station chastized a subordinate for backsliding. The union took reprisals against the engineer, telling other workers to be uncooperative, claiming that the engineer was not a "good compañero." Similarly, a dedicated engineer in an outlying district needed certain supplies to improve efficiency and lower costs. He asked his supervisors, "Where are the supplies?" The supervisor replied, "Come on. We can't get things to you so fast." The engineer protested. Then the supervisor informed him that if he did not calm down, he would be reported to the union, which could punish him for his "undisciplined" attitude. The result was to weaken the motivation and morale of the engineer.

The most distasteful aspect of unionization is the requirement to pay off union heads for employment, promotions, and favorable assignments. In 1975 and 1976 the leaders of the union were as opposed to the incorporation of engineers as were the engineers themselves. Sporadic walk-outs disrupted production as the union leaders made their views known. An agreement was reached whereby the government assured the union bosses that the engineers would not displace them from top union posts. The union then acceded to the entry of the engineers, and soon harvested great benefit from the arrangement. The result was to implicate petroleum engineers in the union's notorious corruption.

Petroleum engineers cannot work for PEMEX unless they join the union, and they must pay off the union leaders to obtain a union card; further, the rule is that they must pay money to the union to be promoted, just as manual workers must. An engineer soon realizes that his career advances in PEMEX owe less to his ability than to his obsequious relationship with union leaders.

Those petroleum engineers who remember "the good old days" commented that a petroleum engineer then was promoted by showing his merit through hard work, experience, scholarly interests, and good judgment. Once the engineers were part of the union, they were placed on a scale *(escalafón)* for their department, unit, and type of job, based purely on seniority. The person who is to be promoted is the oldest in his group, subject to a test of professional competence. In theory, the applicant must take an aptitude examination certifying him for promotion. He has the option of seeking extra training before taking the test. If he does not pass the examination, the second person on the list has a chance, and so on.

In actual practice, the union intervenes in this sequence. For a fee, it suggests that the company not insist on the examination for a certain candidate, claiming that the person already knows everything he needs to know by virtue of his long tenure. The result is often to give a promotion to someone who is incompetent, or to take it away from someone who deserves it.

Union-controlled positions theoretically extend to section heads; *empleados de confianza* refer to department head and above. At that level, the union is not supposed to interfere, but it does anyway. First, it discourages the company from moving qualified individuals laterally to take department head positions. Informants report that union officials say, "Why send us an engineer from elsewhere when we have people right here who can fill the job?" Union resistance makes it difficult for a talented engineer to gain a wide berth of experience in the company. Second, the union encourages engineers promoted to the departmental level *de confianza* not to resign the union, and even to continue paying union dues. In this way, the engineer maintains smooth relations with his subordinates (who otherwise can make his life unpleasant) and can rely on the union to back his orders.

According to many petroleum engineers, the union has contaminated the work environment for professionals working in PEMEX. Indolence, goldbricking, and insubordination have seeped into the profession, and the venal are protected in their habits. It is understandable that conscientious petroleum engineers, who make up the majority, participate enthusiastically in the field's professional associations, where they are evaluated and esteemed by traditionally professional criteria. Neither the union nor the professional associations, however, have allowed petroleum engineers much leeway in regulating the marketplace, certifying professional skills, or increasing their income. Indeed, the union may have had the opposite effect.

THE NATIONAL COLLEGE OF ECONOMISTS

To be successful, a professional association in Mexico would need to be congruent with national values and prevailing structural constraints. Its mission would include placement of members in professional employ, elevation of the stature of the profession, and illumination of the profession's contribution to national issues over a relatively long period and with some indicators of accomplishment. A viable professional organization would be able to maintain group loyalty, recruit outstanding leadership for the association, increase prestige for the profession, and influence public policy issues. Subsidiary activities would maintain professional competence, through seminars and the like. Barring a total transformation of the system, however, the profession would not compete with the state for training, licensing, or regulating professional affairs, given the considerable structural obstacles to doing so effectively.

Of the major professional associations in Mexico, the National College of Economists seems to come closest to matching this description. It has a significant participating membership, it represents a clearinghouse for the employment of economists in the public sector (especially those from the National School of Economics, ENE), and it has succeeded in articulating nationalistic responses to public policy issues. Its leaders have, with occasional exceptions, been democratically elected, and tend to be considered highly talented and prestigious individuals, even by those who do not share their economic thought.

Beginning in the 1960s, the National College of Economists differentiated itself from other professional associations in Mexico by entering more aggressively into the public fray. Its political ideology is statist, and the College has used political economy theory to interpret public policy. By adopting a critical stance toward public policy, while at the same time expressing confidence in the state's ultimate ability to guide the economy toward development, government policymakers have had to engage the College either in direct or indirect debate. The outcome has been either to adopt or to reject the College's position. In either case, the College has been taken seriously, which places it in a different category from other official professional associations.

Still, the College is a controversial organization, and its activities are not appreciated by all economists, especially those who are not graduates of the ENE. Typical critical statements are, "The College of Economists is pure politics."[32] "Go to one of the meetings and look at the membership and the people who attend. It is pathetic. These are persons generally looking for a job."[33] "The College is a political organization that facilitates access to political posts. Its main function is to employ economists . . . Its public policy positions go hand-in-hand with its political and employment functions. I personally am not a member because I don't think it amounts to much."[34]

On the other hand, many economists believe that the College has weight and significance. Formally independent of government, the College allows economists to avoid bureaucratic fights. Economists from public agencies that tend to adopt different views on policy (such as IMCE, the Mexican Institute of Foreign Commerce, and SEPAFIN, the Secretariat of Industries) can meet on neutral ground to discuss their differences in a non-threatening environment. The College opens up the decision-making structure considerably. It provides a forum in which economists can express their views without compromising their bureaucratic positions. The College has tended toward positions on the Left that are "as radical" as the government establishment is likely to countenance. Consequently, when practical judgment requires, the government can adopt the College's position and use the association to legitimate its decision.

The College was at the forefront of the Mexican government's decision not to enter GATT (General Agreement on Tariffs and Trade) in March 1980. The United States at the time was urging Mexican membership as a means of routinizing U.S.-Mexican bilateral trade, with less need for ad hoc tariff concessions and the risk of judicial challenges in U.S. courts. In Mexico, middle-sized industries, labor unions, and economic nationalists believed that GATT would accelerate transnational penetration of the economy and weaken local industry. The College held a number of public and private meetings, and sponsored publicity about the disadvantages of the GATT. Although President López Portillo apparently favored GATT membership, his cabinet was divided. In March 1980, President López Portillo announced three nationalistic measures (oil production ceilings, self-sufficiency in food, postponement of entering GATT), and the College's position was confirmed.[35]

Subsequent to this victory, the College tried to press its advantage, and designed an integral set of nationalistic economic policies. This plan was discussed a year later at the association's meeting in Guadalajara, to which President López Portillo was invited. The President displayed his impatience with the College's pretentiousness, and was eager to prepare the political climate for the announcement of the PRI's next presidential candidate, Miguel de la Madrid, who was considered more free market-oriented in his economic thought. Consequently, the President was highly critical of the College's recommendations.[36] After the selection of de la Madrid, the state openly intervened in the College's October 1981 internal elections. The objective was to assure that the association's leadership would be supportive of PRI's electoral campaign and would not criticize de la Madrid's economic package.

The example reaffirms the inapplicability of a single professional model to explain or evaluate the behavior of Mexican associations. An eclectic approach is more suitable. The College's orientation toward universal membership and yearning for a special relationship with state officials is reminiscent of corporatism. Its advocacy of public policy (namely, state growth), which would be favorable to the gainful employment of its membership, is typical of interest articulation under liberalism. The state's heavy-handed intervention in the College's internal affairs would be standard fare in a centralist system. Other professional associations in Mexico, were they to imitate the College, would face similar ambiguities in their relationships with membership and the state.

CONCLUSIONS

Doctors, lawyers, and engineers in Mexico need to rely on different sorts of organizations to protect their interests than those available to their colleagues elsewhere. Formal Mexican professional associations in these fields are ineffectual in regulating the marketplace, certifying professional competence, defining the boundaries of knowledge in the field, or broadening employment opportunities. The complexity of Mexican history and society is such, however, that the professions have not all developed similar approaches to the pursuit of collective and individual goals. The predominant organizational form in each profession depends on its evolution in the twentieth century, especially in its relations with the state.

Most law students are less interested in litigation than in political and public sector careers. Lawyers are in large supply in government, but few of them are eager to participate in the national bar associations. The appropriate organizational form to defend their interests is the loyalty and friendship group, often called the *camarilla*. A number of *camarillas* compete for advantage within and between each change in presidential administrations. The *camarillas* perpetuate an oliogopolistic system of market control over jobs for lawyers. When successful in appropriating the highest post in the country, that of national president, the *camarilla* can greatly influence public policy. However, *camarillas* do not define relevant knowledge in the field. They maintain a presence in the university mainly to recruit talented students, rather than to absorb new ideas and techniques.

Agronomists rely heavily on school affiliation to differentiate and stratify the profession. Alumni associations might be considered narrow-based *camarillas*, with the additional feature of being more institutional and less personalistic. Indeed, *escuelismo* engenders a sort of credentialism that builds confidence (or wariness) between individuals, even if they have no other reference, aside from school affiliation, on which to base judgments. The allocation of public sector jobs in agronomy depends greatly on the outcome of intense competition among agronomists in the months surrounding presidential elections. Most competent agronomists eventually locate some sort of position, but the coveted high-level jobs accord enormous patronage, and thus are the principal targets of the school groups. Because of their links to the universities, agronomists' alumni associations are more sensitive than are lawyers' organizations to the emergence of new professional techniques, which has an indirect effect on shaping conventional knowledge in the field.

Economists have reinforced and refashioned their official professional association, the National College of Economists, to serve group and member interests. The College has sought the role of the loyal critic of the state's economic policies, and virtually all state ministers dealing in economic affairs are nominal College members. Unlike *camarillas* and alumni associations, the College does not regulate the marketplace for economists. The evolution of the Mexican economy in a capitalistic and technocratic mode has created demands for certain kinds of economists, usually trained abroad, of whom there are relatively few. The College, however, does serve the function of finding junior jobs for young economists through its regular meetings and stimulation of personal relations among members. The College has also elevated the stature of the profession by taking stands on national economic policy, and thus has portrayed economists as key professionals in determining the future of the country.

Peculiar historical events affecting petroleum engineering and medicine in Mexico have smothered attempts to create semi-autonomous professional organizations. Ironically, the distaste of many PEMEX petroleum engineers for their obligatory union membership induces them to seek refuge in the two prestige and social associations in the field. Neither of these associations, however, regulates the professional marketplace or influences public policy. For their part, doctors have been frustrated in their attempts to define the profession's place in Mexican society. Professional cleavages result from the multiplicity of state health service agencies, the prevalence of moonlighting among doctors, the trend toward medical specializations (each with its own association), and the status differential between those privileged professionals with remunerative positions and the large numbers of resentful, unemployed doctors. Moreover, the state has been wary of blurring these distinctions for fear of a renewed political movement among doctors, such as the one in 1965. While the National Academy has established norms for the minimal knowledge required for practicing specialities, passing the Academy's test is honorific and not obligatory for a doctor to call himself a specialist. Consequently, doctors have no organizational mechanism to create employment, influence public policy, or control standards in the profession.

CHAPTER 5
Professions and the State

Future historians chronicling the emergence of Mexican professions may categorize their current stage as the era of preconsciousness. Several basic conditions for professional consolidation exist, but they are not widely perceived as such. Except perhaps in the case of law, the factors have not been shaped into a "professional project" achievable under the logic of the Mexican system.[1] The project, of course, implies a different strategy from those characteristic of liberal systems, where professional development occurred in civil society and involved independent associational bodies acting on the state. Although Mexico cannot be called a purely corporatist or centralist system, it does share many of the traits associated with those systems as they pertain to professional autonomy, privilege, and prestige. More so than in England or the United States, examples of professional development in France and Germany are salient for Mexico. Mexican professions, to be successful, must consciously address their relations with the state. To the degree that they are absorbed by the state, while carving out their authority within it, the project will near completion.[2]

Several factors facilitate or constrain the Mexican professional project. The nature of the Mexican system impedes the emergence of liberal professions. Simultaneously, it gives favorable access to individual professionals with skills necessary for managing the polity, while holding the role of traditional power contenders (labor, business) relatively constant. The maturation of protective

[87]

organizations (such as alumni associations and bureaucratic unions) has provided the current generation of professionals with useful political experience. The university system has collaborated by creating a large body of professionals from which to recruit and seek reciprocal support. In many institutions, professionals are a filter for hiring, which is a means of regulating the marketplace. Professionals' high prestige on Mexico's occupational scale means that society expects them to play leading roles. The gradual entry into senior political posts by representatives of different professions is a further demonstration of professional advancement.

These various factors have not yet coalesced, in part because of liberal perceptions of the "proper" role of professions, a perception that is stronger in some fields (medicine, petroleum engineering) than in others, and in part because of incomplete awareness among professional leaders that professional consolidation requires a conscious plan. Critics who view professions as perpetuating social inequality will not lament their failure to achieve their vested interests. They can take solace in the fact that the eventual direction of professional consolidation is difficult to predict, and may not occur at all, especially if certain subsidiary trends prevail.[3]

PROFESSIONS AND POLICYMAKING

The academic literature on technocrats alludes to the political power of professionals, despite the fact that the terms are not interchangeable. A professional is a legitimately licensed member of an occupation considered by fiat or custom to be a profession. Technocrats are specialists with public sector jobs that require advanced knowledge and training.[4] Politicized professionals in civil society spend the major portion of their working lives in various specialized occupations outside the party, mass organizations, and the state administration (such as tenured positions in the universities); for these professionals, "politics is an avocation."[5] Politicians follow a political career path that potentially encompasses many different official and semi-official posts in the system, and which transcends fields of specialized knowledge. A politician need never have been a technocrat or a professional, and a technocrat does not necessarily need to hold a professional degree. In Mexico, however, the various categories are increasingly intermingled.

While students of bureaucracy observe that technocrats wield power, they disagree on the source of that power. Ezra Suleiman's data from France do not support the contention that technocracy is synonymous with rationality, that it is based on common educational and class ties, or that it is characterized by homogenous behavior.[6] Merilee Grindle finds academic defenders of the somewhat contrary viewpoints that the power of the technocrat derives from his expertise or from his political superiors, or that technocrats are altogether inconsequential in policy initiation.[7] Her own assessment is that the successful Mexican technocrat combines "technically related skills with astute political insights and abilities," and that it usually is difficult to distinguish clearly between the technocrat and the politician.[8] Thomas Baylis, in studying East Germany, makes the significant point that the power of the technical intelligentsia depends on its *awareness* of the power realities of the political system and on its *consciousness* of its own potential power.[9] Mexican professionals, except for lawyers, generally lack this subjective assertiveness.

The contention that Mexican professions (except law) are in a state of preconsciousness is illustrated by their fervent denial of political efficacy. Professionals in various fields disclaim much influence over policy formation, even though objective analysis locates parallels between professional interests and the contours of public policy. To be sure, certain professions are better able than others to mold the definition of policy problems and how to address them. The order of professional political power among fields examined in this book, from the weakest to the strongest, is petroleum engineering, medicine, agronomy, economics, and law. Furthermore, the complexity and opaqueness of the Mexican political system make it difficult to pinpoint the exact forces acting on major decisions, and gives some credence to professional denials. Professionals nonetheless have more influence than they readily admit.

Petroleum engineers are technicians who work with sophisticated machinery, often in isolated areas away from contact with most of the Mexican population. As years separate them from their university days and they participate increasingly in their professional associations, they speak more self-assuredly about desirable public policy in the energy sector. They feel their direct influence on policy formation, however, to be tangential, limited to project specifications and implementation. Petroleum policy is decided directly by the President, with some advice from the director of PEMEX. The President and PEMEX director in turn are buffeted by a broad spectrum of political and economic factors, including the need to use oil for budgetary revenues, domestic industrialization plans, balance of payments relief, foreign policy initiatives, or a nationalistic symbol.

Doctors are the largest single group of professionals within the state. Junior doctors in the public health agencies work under stringent guidelines dictating how many patients they must treat per hour. Doctors feel that the definition of productivity (patient load) detracts from the quality of the doctor/patient relationship, and incurs occasional diagnostic or surgical errors. While the treatment in public health institutes usually is adequate, job satisfaction among the twenty thousand public health doctors does not seem to be high. As in a factory, doctors are required to punch time cards when they arrive for work, and punch out at the end of the day.

Doctors feel they wield little collective or individual influence in setting health policy, and they often are cynical about their inefficacy. They feel their participation in high-level politics is token, limited to devising ways of attending to eligible members of the social security system or drawing up a list of generic medicines, rather than determining the level of resources applied to preventive, out-patient, or hospital care. It is the "politicians" who make health policy by responding to outside pressure and accommodating the wishes of the doctors.[10]

Doctors cite as molders of health policy the pharmaceutical companies (in promoting curative, drug-related medicine), private sector contractors (who want to build more clinics and hospitals), the purchasing agencies in the health institutes (which permit leakage of state funds into private hands), the workers insured under the IMSS, ISSSTE, and PEMEX (who insist on monopolizing quality medicine for themselves even though they are a minority in the nation as a whole), and, from time to time, the International Monetary Fund (which insists that Mexico spend less on social services to reduce the public sector budgetary deficit).[11]

Agronomists are specialists in soils, plagues, insects, irrigation, or seeds, and the state employs them in these capacities. Agronomists are quick to deny that they have had much overall influence since the government of Plutarco Calles (1924-1928). They note that irrigation policy historically has dominated Mexican agricultural development, and agronomists were not consulted on where to place the dams and how to distribute the water. Furthermore, if given the opportunity, agronomists would have sponsored a different agrarian reform with less deleterious effects on land distribution and agricultural productivity. Lawyers and economists, not agronomists, decide the annual agricultural budget. Agronomists claim that politicians accept the agronomist's point of view only so long as he agrees with the politician on basic policy and limits his input to details. The Secretary of Agriculture, who is seldom an agronomist, asks professional advice on purely technical matters, and agronomists' influence is confined to these spheres.[12]

If the agronomists do not determine agricultural policy, who does? Agronomists point to the civil engineers (who were instrumental in building irrigation dams and canals in the 1940s and 1950s, and who control water distribution to the present day), large commercial farmers in the northwest and northeast (often in alliance with the civil engineers), leaders of the National Confederation of Peasants in Congress (who manifest their points of view to the President and the Secretary of Agriculture), BANRURAL (in determining agricultural credit policy), state governors (by advocating federal agricultural schemes in their states), and consumers (by preferring certain kinds of beans and corn over others). This mishmash of interests leads an agronomist to exclaim, "I don't know who directs agricultural policy. I don't see them. Maybe they don't exist."[13] He was certain, however, that the policymakers are not agronomists.

The majority of the state's economists are engaged in cost-benefit analysis, project design, feasibility studies, budget preparation and accounting, and projections of economic trends. This activity draws on their university training, and relates to policy implementation. Senior economists, however, join the chorus of fellow professionals who claim they have virtually no influence on policy initiation. Economists feel that while they may influence the technical aspects of national problems, major decisions are taken in the political sphere, which "swallows the issue, digests it, and regurgitates it as a government program."[14] Economists have greater leeway in influencing economic policy to the degree that a larger number of political groups are pressuring to advance their own positions. Economists can play the role of arbiter, so that the ultimate decision is more or less a function of economic considerations. But economists do not feel this input adds up to effective guidance of economic policy. Although economists have earned more responsibility in economic matters, the decisions are in the hands of politicians.

To purists, economists appointed to high posts are not economists. Rather, they become politicians with a relative commitment to promoting decisions based on economic criteria. Even these technocrats are upstaged. Professionals like to cite the famous phrase Echeverría is said to have mouthed when Hugo Margáin was replaced by López Portillo: "It makes no difference who is the Secretary of Finance; I'm the one who runs the show!"

Politicians mediate and modulate the pressure from various groups in society, including business groups' official representative organs (CONCAMIN, CANACINTRA), labor officials (from the CTM and Congress of Labor), multinational corporations, and the President.

Most lawyers in the state employ are low-level administrators. They interact with petitioners and apply existing regulations in the Secretariat of Government (Interior), strive to achieve accommodations in the Secretariat of Work between workers and employers, and manage land titles in agrarian reform to reduce the level of rural conflict. They become experts in procedures and their discretion is exercised on a case-by-case basis, rather than in setting general policy. Once they arrive in high posts, however, the perception is that they wield power. Although lawyers may feel that their influence is slipping, most would concur with the lawyer who expressed confidence in the profession's continuing weight:

> You ask, 'What political influence do lawyers have in Mexico?' The answer is 100 percent. They have had a monopoly on the political direction of the country since 1946 . . . Today in Mexico lawyers occupy the Presidency, the head of the Chamber of Deputies and the Senate, and the head of the Supreme Court. Thus lawyers lead the three major branches of government.[15]

The hubris of lawyers is refreshing when virtually all other professionals deny that they wield any political influence at all. Professionals' self-effacement, however, is unconvincing for two reasons: (1) major directions in Mexican state policy in each of these sectors has been in the interests of significant elements within these professions, and (2) examples *do* exist of policies adopted on the basis of overt intervention of individuals motivated by professional criteria.

Petroleum engineers may feel they have not been consulted on certain aspects of PEMEX's oil policies, but the general thrust of these actions has furthered the engineers' interests. Petroleum engineers are trained to find and pump oil. Nationalistic bidding procedures prior to 1976 helped raise their expertise to world-class levels. Aggressive exploration and oil field development after 1976 permitted full expression of their professional raison d'être. Doctors' complaints about lack of direct participation in health policy ignores the fact that current Mexican approaches to medicine favor biological methods relying on prescription drugs, specialization, and hospital beds. The approach caters to the preferences of the great majority of doctors, who were trained in this school and who find it compatible with their private practices and relations with colleagues abroad.

Agronomy and economics are split between the divergent approaches to their fields described in Chapter 2. The state's agricultural policy since the 1940s has favored "agricultural modernization," which corresponds to the dominant wing of the agronomic profession.[16] Under López Portillo, two seemingly contradictory agricultural policies were promulgated—one facilitating private commercial farming on *ejido* lands, which favors the modernizers' point of view, and the other favoring more equitable income distribution in the countryside, the use of farmland for basic grains (maize and beans), and higher nutritional standards among consumers, which favors the campesinistas' point of view.[17] While agronomists' role in drafting the legislation was sporadic, the positions corresponded closely to each group's implicit preferences for the future of Mexican agriculture.[18]

The prevailing economic policy during most of the López Portillo and de la Madrid governments was neoclassical. Nationalistic or statist economists were kept off stage. The 1982 international debt crisis required new policy approaches, as much for political as for economic reasons. The nationalization of the private, Mexican-owned banking system was advocated and executed by statist economists fully representative of their wing of the profession.[19]

In summary, professionals in Mexico typically influence policy by (a) establishing a national agenda for policy debate, (b) determining the methodology for analysis, (c) generating relevant data for decision-making, and (d) exercising discretion during implementation. That some of them occasionally initiate and execute policy is supplementary proof of their importance.

PROFESSIONALS AS POLITICIANS

Another way of gauging the rise of professionals in the state is by their concentrated presence in public institutions. In 1970 Mexico conducted a census of the general population, and in 1975 of centralized and decentralized state agencies.[20] The percentage of respondents describing their occupations as professional or technical was 5.65 percent for the work force as a whole, 34.3 percent for employees of central state agencies, and 19.3 percent for employees of decentralized agencies. Although 1.4 million state workers made up only 10.8 percent of the economically active population in 1970, professionals working in the public sector constituted more than half of all professionals in the country.[21]

These data can be further broken down by specialty. In the centralized sector of government, the total professional cadre can be ordered by the percentage in each field. Lawyers led the list with 12.35 percent of all professionals, followed by doctors (10.99), civil engineers (10.69), accountants (9.64), mechanical and electrical engineers (6.94), public administrators (6.92), economists (4.83), and agronomists (4.83). Petroleum engineers and geologists were 29th on the list of 33 professions, representing 0.4 percent of the overall group.[22] In the decentralized sector, doctors were the most prevalent (16.14 percent), followed by accountants (13.79), mechanical and electrical engineers (13.61), lawyers (7.10), civil engineers (6.64), administrators (6.52), chemical engineers (4.88), economists (4.57), chemists and druggists (3.69), industrial engineers (3.0), architects (2.95), dentists (2.49), agronomists (2.25), and petroleum engineers and geologists (1.49).[23]

While the vast majority of these self-identified *profesionistas y técnicos* had not fully completed their university degrees, it is safe to conclude that the state is the major employer of professionals in Mexico and that the state's access to technical expertise is increasing yearly. Table 3 indicates the total number of doctors, lawyers, economists, agronomists, and extraction engineers working in both the centralized and decentralized sectors, and indicates the percentage that had finished their licenciate degrees in 1975.

High-level decision-making posts traditionally have been filled by lawyers, who have dominated membership in the political elite of Mexico. Peter Smith finds that lawyers made up 44.4 percent of the top elite in the 1900-1911 period, 37.8 percent in 1917-1940, and 47.1 percent in 1946-1971.[24] The PRI's presidential candidate is recruited from these ranks, and lawyers have had a virtual lock on the presidency since the political system put aside military leaders in the Cárdenas administration. Avila Camacho (1940-1946) was the last military man to become president, and he was followed by lawyers Miguel Alemán (1946-1952), Aldolfo López Mateos (1958-1964), Gustavo Díaz Ordaz (1964-1970), Luis Echeverría Alvarez (1970-1976), José López Portillo (1976-1982), and Miguel de la Madrid Hurtado (1982-1988).[25] The earlier presidents on this list were prone to appoint lawyers to political posts. From 1917 to 1971, "out of every five lawyers who entered the national political elite, about two could expect to reach the upper pinnacles of prominence," an extraordinary success rate.[26]

Table 3 Public Sector Professionals, 1975

Professions	Total	Percentage of all professionals in state employment	Licenciate degree completed	%	Licenciate degree not completed	%
Medicine	19,050	13.4	14,750	77.4	4,300	22.6
Law	14,077	9.9	9,631	68.4	4,446	31.6
Economics	6,696	4.7	4,414	65.9	2,282	34.1
Agronomy	4,546	3.2	4,050	89.1	496	10.9
Extractive engineering	1,191	0.8	1,013	85.1	178	14.9

Note: The total number of public sector employees in 1975 was 1,398,410, divided between the central ministries (55.2 percent) and state enterprises and decentralized institutions (44.8 percent).

Source: Mexico, *Censo de recursos humanos del sector público federal: administración central 1975* (Mexico City: Comisión de Recursos Humanos del Gobierno Federal, 1976), p. 60; Mexico, *Censo de recursos humanos del sector público federal: administración decentralizado y de participación estatal mayoritaria 1975* (Mexico City: Comisión de Recursos Humanos del Gobierno Federal, 1976), p. 165.

This trend, however, is altering. Table 4 demonstrates an erosion of lawyers' dominant possession of cabinet posts. While lawyers occupied 52.9 percent of these positions at the beginning of the López Mateos government, the figure dropped to 16.7 percent by the conclusion of the López Portillo administration. A field that fell completely from favor under López Portillo was engineering. At the end of his administration, the non-lawyers were economists (4), Ph.D. scientists (3), military men (2), school teachers (2), and a doctor, an agronomist, an architect, and an accountant.

Although lawyers appeared to regain ground in de la Madrid's first cabinet, the percentage figure must be interpreted cautiously. Three of the seven lawyers were holdovers from previous administrations whose appointments broadened political support for de la Madrid. Moreover, the sub-cabinet levels of the public sector were filled with widely diverse professionals — MBAs, accountants, communications and public administration graduates — many with degrees from private Mexican universities followed by graduate studies abroad. This hierarchical level consists of the main contenders for the next generation of cabinet secretaries.

Table 4 The Displacement of Lawyers as Cabinet Ministers, 1958-1982

Cabinet Ministers by Profession (N)[a]	López Mateos 1958	López Mateos 1964	Diaz Ordaz 1964	Diaz Ordaz 1970	Echeverria 1970	Echeverria 1976	López Portillo 1976	López Portillo 1982	De la Madrid 1982
Lawyers	9	8	8	7	6	8	6	3	7
Engineers	1	2	3	5	4	5	0	0	1
Doctors	1	1	2	2	1	1	1	1	1
Military	1	1	2	2	2	2	2	2	2
Other Professionals[b]	3	4	3	2	4	3	8	11	8
Nonprofessionals	2	2	0	0	1	0	1	1	0
Total	17	18	18	18	18	19	18	18	19
Lawyer Ministers (%)	52.9	44.4	44.4	38.9	33.3	42.1	33.3	16.7	36.8

Notes: [a]Cabinet ministers include secretaries of Interior, Attorney General's Office, Foreign Relations, Defense, Navy, Treasury, Planning and Budgeting (beginning 1976), Industries, Commerce (beginning 1976), Hydraulic Resources (until 1976), Agriculture, Communications and Transport (beginning 1958), Public Works, Education, Health, Labor, Agrarian Reform, Tourism (beginning 1974), Government Property (until 1976), Presidency (until 1976), Fishing (beginning 1982), and Federal District Department.

[b]Includes economists, agronomists, architects, social and basic scientists, accountants, school teachers, and MBAs.

Source: Most of the information for this table comes from Roderic A. Camp, *Mexican Political Biographies: 1935-1975* (Tucson: University of Arizona Press, 1976).

Lawyers are alarmed by their displacement. While lawyers might accept that an economist heads the Bank of Mexico, they do not abdicate proprietary rights over the Secretariat of Finance, which has as many legal as financial functions. Lawyers feel that doctors, agronomists, and economists should restrict their activities to technical functions, and leave administrative responsibilities to them. The cardiologist, for instance, should not be distracted from saving lives to outline health plans, for which he has no training. Similarly, a state minister does not need to be an expert on drip irrigation to design agricultural policy.[27]

The reasons for the increased presence of professionals in the Mexican cabinet with training other than law are myriad. The large number of professionally trained individuals in diverse fields creates constituencies to which the political system must respond. Appointments of agronomists, school teachers, doctors, economists, and engineers to high posts provides a vicarious feeling of efficacy and participation to segments of the body politic that are alienated from one-party politics. The high-level technocrat is a kind of nominated deputy for segments of the upper middle class in a political system where the legislature is a democratic artifice. The trend could be considered a subsidiary manifestation of collective professional co-optation, as contrasted with the more common sort of individual co-optation involving direct or indirect material gain.

Lawyers have placed excessive faith in their generalist education and *camarilla* networks as a means of holding onto top jobs, and have been lackadaisical in self-regulation against corruption. As a result, their prestige has fallen among other professional groups and among the private entrepreneurial classes. While businessmen may feel grateful that Mexico is not spending a large percentage of its GNP on military hardware, they increasingly feel that the advantage is mostly lost when such extraordinary sums are channelled into public sector corruption. Thus lawyers have fewer defenders in Mexican society, and other types of professionals, with a less negative reputation, have gradually broken the lawyers' hold on top political posts.

The management of the Mexican state has become more complicated, and now requires personnel with sophisticated technical skills. Individuals who are conversant in these techniques have gradually concentrated in relevant ministries, the obvious cases being doctors in the health sector, agronomists and hydraulic specialists in agriculture, and civil engineers and architects in public works. Political careers in Mexico are such that promotion within the sector to a ministerial post is uncommon. But the appointment of a professional with political skills to a high position in the sectoral ministry which corresponds to his training enhances the state's technical competence and its ability to maintain smooth relations with its functionaries.

Professionals in nonjuridical realms are increasingly more capable than lawyers to contribute to the three implicit functions of the Mexican state: ideological symbology, economic growth, and social control. Economists propose formulas for economic well-being while stealing the podium from lawyers in debates on issues of nationalism. School teachers are instrumental in transmitting symbols of national identity to new generations of school-age Mexicans (in a country where almost half of the population is under 15 years of age). Teachers are on location throughout the national republic, including poor rural and urban areas where educational facilities have increasingly spread and where cause for social dissent is most objectively real. Political elites recognize that the military is the ultimate enforcer of social peace; it has played that role faithfully in the past. System defenders believe that the military should be close to the pinnacle of power when its services are again in demand, as they most likely will be.

The erosion of the lawyers' monopoly on high-level posts is a fact. It is unlikely, however, that this trend will much change the way power is exercised in Mexico. The legal profession has traditionally been coidentified with politics, and politics with the practice of law. Lawyers' success to date has been due to their skills in negotiation, accommodation, and persuasion, and to the fact that they have been able to synthesize the technical biases of other professionals into integrated government actions. The challenge for other professionals is to imitate the success of the lawyers, rather than to reject it. Indeed, as nonjuridical professionals have moved up the hierarchy they have tended to deemphasize their professional origins and to accentuate their political skills. Other professions, including those based on rigorously scientific premises, will perfect these capabilities as they become more accustomed to holding positions of authority.

A successful professional project in Mexico implies capturing relevant portions of the state apparatus, which can be used as a bastion for defensive and offensive operations. Of the technical professions studied here, only the economists appear to be gaining proprietary rights to the leadership of state institutions in their field, such as the Bank of Mexico, Nacional Financiera, and the secretariats of Finance and National Properties. The doctors, agronomists, and petroleum engineers still have not laid sustained claim to the leadership of institutions in their fields, such as the national health institutes, the Secretariat of Agriculture and Water Resources, or PEMEX. Filling intermediate posts is a necessary first step toward capturing the bureaucracy and permits incremental political gains. When the political system honors the profession's ongoing claim to politically important posts, the project is nearly complete. The prize, however, is not just waiting to be taken. Technocrats face competition from other constituencies, such as business, labor, and agriculture, and of course from the lawyers themselves.

PROFESSIONAL TRENDS IN MEXICO

In light of these considerations, what trends are likely to persist in the evolution of the Mexican professions, and which may represent departures from past patterns?

First, over the medium term, the Mexican state will continue to exert a preponderant weight on professional affairs. As groups, professions' enforceable demands on the political system will be limited to relatively low-level labor matters (especially for doctors) in state institutions. As professionals of different types gradually occupy more top-level public sector positions, their influence on policy through agenda–setting and implementation will become more pervasive. Over time, if they succeed in consolidating their proprietary rights over state agencies, professional orientations will become one means by which the Mexican state exercises its relative autonomy over powerful class interests in civil society.

Second, the "massification" of professional education may level off, but will not decline. The cohort of poorly trained and/ or unemployed professionals from public universities will increase in size. Academically qualified students (mainly from upper-class backgrounds) will seek (and find) alternate routes to professional education, including private universities and graduate studies either in Mexico or abroad. Exclusionary patterns within the professions (now affecting economics, medicine, and some engineering fields) will extend to such other areas as agronomy and petroleum engineering. A minority of students from more privileged backgrounds will be the ones who locate professional employment, while the majority never complete their studies and find no jobs in their fields. Clientele networks leading to professional jobs will relocate to private universities, thus further dampening the prospects for poor students in the public universities to obtain a foothold in the system. Student protests over the lack of professional jobs, which have been practically nonexistent to date, may be a matter to reckon with in the future.

Third, formal professional associations will continue to be ineffective organs for professional expression, solidarity, and policy advocacy. Informal parallel networks, such as the university alumni club, will provide the main sources of protection and advancement for individual professionals. These subsystems, with distinct features in each field, will exercise a stabilizing effect on professsional anxiety in the preconsciousness stage. Doctors' unions within the health institutes will focus professional attention on work-related grievances. The state is unlikely to promote a unification of health service agencies, in part to avoid the specter of a nationwide doctors' union, which would represent a potentially formidable political force. Similarly, it is improbable that petroleum engineers will win a quick release from their obligatory membership in the PEMEX workers' union. National officials will continue to fear that a separate professional association would gain the ability to disrupt oil production, on which the national economy is increasingly dependent. The professional associations in the field will offer a refuge for conscientious petroleum engineers to interact socially, but these loose groupings are unlikely to advocate public policy positions that counter the government's approach to exploration, exploitation, pricing, and exports.

Fourth, the nationalistic values now typical of some professions will weaken. New generations of practitioners will be neither knowledgeable of nor socialized in the revolutionary principles that pervaded agronomy, economics, and petroleum engineering at their inception in Mexico. These notions will seem increasingly anachronistic and quaint. Attractive international techniques will further penetrate the fields, with little competition from homegrown methodologies, which will have difficulty proving their relevance and efficiency. A greater incidence of postgraduate training abroad may make professionals less, rather than more, capable of using their training to solve uniquely Mexican problems. After an era of technocracy, however, lawyers may find that their approaches to problem-solving are revalued, as they are called upon to formulate suitable and sensible policies for Mexican development. To play this role, lawyers and others will need to help redefine a concept of the Mexican Revolution.

Fifth, existing prestige ratings of the professions are likely to remain steady, with some adjustments. In the abstract, the prestige and illusion of high income of professional occupations will continue to draw large numbers of students to the university. Mexicans will be more able to distinguish between the professional specialties, even the newer ones, and come to judgments on which deserve deference for their contributions to society. Leaders of the law profession will want to take stock of its declining reputation in Mexican society, and attempt to refurbish its image from within. Conscientious lawyers will need to confront eventually the issue of corruption, although the difficulty in eradicating or even attenuating it is enormous, given its function in co-optation.

Doctors currently suffer a wide discrepancy between their social prestige and political power. While the state would not permit a unification of doctors, it is likely that more doctors will be recruited into top-level government positions as a way to mollify resentment over the truncated political influence of doctors. A status incongruity also affects agronomists, whose training is sophisticated and for whom job opportunities (at least for the moment) are plentiful. Yet barring some unusual turn of events (like an erudite agronomist becoming a popular and skillful President of the Republic), other professionals will continue in their condescending attitudes. Economists' prestige appears to be on an upward swing, despite their uneven training, redundancy in numbers, and nagging questions about their ability to manage the economy. If they consolidate their hold on key state agencies, their social prestige is likely to rise. The competition among professionals for prestige and income, however, is not such that this segment of the Mexican elite is subject to severe splits and dissension. The Mexican state, with its pyramidal structure and clientele linkages, appears to be unified at its peak.[28]

Sixth, the military's professional competence is growing yearly. New generations of military officers are trained not just in the use of war matériel but in economic planning, engineering, history, and sociology. The military is an opaque force in Mexican society and its membership is not large, yet it commands the organization, resources, and unity that other professional groups lack.[29] Moreover, it yearns for more status after several decades of ostracism. Should political continuity be disrupted, the military would be waiting in the wings to take center political stage. The losers would be the lawyers/politicians (among others), and the military probably represents a more serious threat to lawyers' influence than do economists, engineers, or doctors.

Seventh, professional leadership will face difficulties reconciling the ethical standards of professionals in civil society with behavior characteristic of upper-level Mexican bureaucracy.

The most articulate professional leaders in Mexico cite as criteria of professionalism a commitment to social justice, rationality and efficiency, abstinence from illicit public sector gain, a strong work ethic, development of techniques suited to national problems, and methods to insure multi-class recruitment into the professional ranks. If professionals ignore these objectives while entrenching themselves in positions of bureaucratic power, increased "professionalism" will have ambiguous connotations for Mexican society.

Gradual differentiation and pluralism are constant features of Mexican society, and are reflected in part in the development of modern professions. The political system is forever adjusting its methods of social control and incorporation to manage new demands and account for new contingencies. There is little reason to predict that professionalization will induce a significant change in the way the state or the class system behaves.[30] For the immediate future, professionals will be obliged to contribute to state goals in ways determined primarily by the state. The professions' main challenge is to become more consistently part of the state, and thus to help mold its future evolution. Professionalization will thus reinforce political patterns in Mexico, rather than mark a departure toward radically new forms of social organization, interest group activity, and public policy.

PROFESSIONS AND THE STATE

The social sciences have suggested alternative analytical models for understanding Third World states, but just one model for professions. This book's purpose has not been to outline systematic new theory on the emergence of professions, but it is apparent that many of the characteristics of professions in liberal capitalistic societies (which most current theory purports to describe) do not exist in most Third World countries.

Social and political history govern the development of professions. In liberal capitalistic systems, the nationalistic origins of the professions have gradually been supplemented by scientific and technical methodologies that enhance the professions' claim to universality, even though their approaches and knowledge base still are most relevant to their own societies. The political system operates on a notion of "balancing interests" and the pursuit of narrow or self-centered objectives is considered normal. The major universities jealously guard their standards and avoid massive enrollments. Professionals and professional groups articulate policy alternatives with little fear of retribution.

Their recommendations are rooted in their own self-interest, but they often are justified plausibly by a notion of the social good.

Salient aspects of Third World societies are the expression of nationalism, the modern role of the university, and the evolution of state-society relations. Professionals in many countries are subjected to the tensions of nationalism versus internationalism. Professions in advanced countries have been able to externalize their influence through training, exchange, and research output; they attract many of the most talented professionals from poor countries, who are distracted from applying their creativity to purely national issues. Nationalists in the wings of the profession at home seek to discredit their internationalist compatriots, either on principle or to gain advantage in the local society. This competition further weakens the professions' internal cohesion, and prolongs their consolidation in national society.

The national university system is a key actor in the process. Its influence on professional orientations depends on its location in two dimensions: elite versus massive enrollment, and nationalist versus internationalist training. Two distinguishing features of professional education in nineteenth-century liberal capitalist societies were its elitist and nationalistic biases. The course curriculum addressed national problems, and student matriculation was limited. By contrast, the typical pattern in many public universities in Latin America (and elsewhere) in the 1960s and early 1970s was a massive-internationalist approach in the basic sciences and technical professions, and a massive-nationalist approach in the social sciences and humanities, with little research in either. For example, the knowledge bases of fields like biology and medicine tended to be imported, archaic, and unrelated to national problems. In economics, however, classroom activities were dominated by unrigorous marxist interpretations of national problems, and in law by formalistic memorization of the country's jurisprudence. Massification diluted criteria for excellence and undermined a commitment to research. The decline in quality produced a reaction in some countries. Elitist-internationalist education has characterized Chilean university programs since the 1973 military coup, and also training at some licenciate and post graduate programs elsewhere. In extreme cases, a relatively small number of students pursue professional training inspired by the world's leading centers of learning, with only tangential relevance for their own societies.

No Latin American university has structured professional training and research around nationalistic reference points while restricting entry to only the most qualified secondary students. Nationalistic professional training (which is conversant with but not beholden to international trends), an insistence on high quality indigenous research, and an adequate matching of the number of graduates with available jobs would be means of raising standards and providing relevant training. Restrictions on university entrance, however, would eliminate an important social function of some university systems (and, indirectly, the professions themselves) of clouding the awareness of lower class youth that their aspirations for mobility are unrealistic.

Once professionals receive a qualifying degree, their organizations evolve consistent with the ways society satisfies requirements for mutual protection, career advancement, and material gain. If region or ethnicity attracts the primary loyalty of individuals, professional alliances will follow suit. If school affiliation or social class contacts prevail, the "real" professional association will reflect these forces. Only rarely will conditions be propitious for professionals to organize in relatively impersonal, goal-oriented, interest-aggregating formal structures defending the long-term aims of the collectivity.

Attributes of professions in liberal capitalistic societies contribute to the wealth of classes and of the nation as a whole, and therefore are supportive of the class structure. These characteristics would change if professions did not add to economic accumulation, and would not survive long if they opposed the logic of the political system. For example, the features of professionalism in Mexico described in this book are supportive of maintaining a harmonious social order that is largely in the interests of the economic, social, and political elites. In analyzing the role of professionals anywhere, it is important to ascertain the power relations operating in society and to examine professionals' place within those relations. While professionals may subscribe to higher standards of excellence and social responsibility than do other occupational groups, they invariably enter into a compact with the existing power structure, within which they can represent a conscience or an agent of change, but rarely a revolutionary force. In this sense, professional "autonomy" is relative. Where professional groups are stable they are a reflection of the social system. Only in times of upheaval or the deliberate formation of national identity can professionals be expected to espouse perspectives that are widely divergent from established patterns.

Many countries are characterized by strong state sectors. To the degree that the state is hegemonic, liberal professional autonomy will be curtailed and professionals will be subjected to the state's demands. Professionals need not despair, however, because governments appoint professionals to public sector posts, where they have the opportunity to mold conditions creating income, privilege, and prestige. The individual professional does not seek autonomy vis-à-vis his employer or client. Rather, the administrative unit obtains collective autonomy for all its professionals through bureaucratic politics within the state apparatus. Autonomy is characterized by interaction and collaboration with other professionals in self-defined social tasks—for example, the design and implementation of a public works plan—and involves discretion in recruitment and promotion. Unlike an ideal liberal system, in which the state often endows professions with monopoly over occupational activities in the marketplace, in a state-dominated system the state accords privilege directly to professions by virtue of their special classification in the administrative career ladder.[31] As for prestige, bureaucratic barriers help keep professional blemishes out of the public eye. Professional leaders can more easily project a unified image of competence, social responsibility, and high ethical standards to society at large, thus reinforcing the profession's status. These various missions, however, are incomplete until the profession solidifies its position in the state apparatus.

In any social system, professional leadership faces the challenge of articulating a historical interpretation of the role of professions and of a set of standards for desirable behavior. These concepts are most successful when they are based on notions of social service, professional ethics, and criteria of excellence that are charismatically molded to the unique features of the nation. To persevere and prosper, professions must eventually obtain an organizational bastion from which to operate. However, the ultimate explanation for the persistence of professions is that some occupations have consistently demonstrated that their contributions to society exceed their members' compensation in terms of superior prestige, authority, and income. The compact between professions and society is always under review, is temporally bound, and is liable to be discarded when trust is betrayed or its utility exhausted. Professionals must strive continuously to insure that their contribution to social betterment resembles the myths they propagate.

Notes

CHAPTER 1: MEXICAN PROFESSIONS COMPARED

1. Debate over definitions of the state is extensive. In this study, the notion of state is pragmatic, referring to political leadership and public organizations. Civil society is conceived to be the classes, groups, and individuals that in varying degrees contribute to, receive benefits from, and challenge the workings of the state. For a full analysis of these concepts, see Alfred C. Stepan, *State and Society* (Princeton: Princeton University Press, 1978), chapter 1. For their utility in analyzing policy-making and the state apparatus, including the concept of relative autonomy of the state, see Peter S. Cleaves and Martin J. Scurrah, *Agriculture, Bureaucracy and Military Government in Peru* (Ithaca: Cornell University Press, 1980), chapters 1 and 8. A general discussion of the Mexican political system is found in Roger D. Hansen, *The Politics of Mexican Development* (Baltimore: Johns Hopkins University Press, 1971), and Alan Riding, *Distant Neighbors* (New York: Alfred A. Knopf, 1985).

2. The more important works include Alexander Morris Carr-Saunders and P. A. Wilson, *The Professions* (London: Oxford University Press, 1933); Talcott Parsons, "Professions," in David L. Sills (ed), *International Encyclopedia of the Social Sciences* (New York: Crowell, Collier and Macmillan, 1968), pp. 536–547; Terence J. Johnson, *Professions and Power* (London: Macmillan, 1972); Geoffrey Millerson, *The Qualifying Associations* (London: Routledge and Kegan Paul, 1964); and Magali Sarfatti Larson, *The Rise of Professionalism* (Berkeley: University of California Press, 1977).

3. Eliot Freidson notes that the term "profession is intrinsically bound up with a peculiar period of history and with only a limited number of nations in that period of history." See "The Theory of Professions: State of the Art," in Robert Dingwell and Philip Lewis, eds., *The Sociology of the Professions: Doctors, Lawyers, and Others* (New York: St. Martin's Press, 1982), p. 26. Among

the few studies of Mexican professions are Pablo Latapí, "Profesiones y sociedad," unpublished article, Prospectiva Universitaria, 1982; Isidoro del Camino y Jorge Muñoz B., "La enseñanza profesional en México en 1970," *Revista del Centro de Estudios Educativos* 2:3 (1972), pp. 125-165; Ingrid Rosenblüeth, "Dependencia tecnológica e involución profesional: la industria y la ingeniería química en México," *Relaciones: Estudios de Historia y Sociedad* I:1 (Winter 1980), pp. 35-90; and Guillermo Villaseñor García, "Una visión estructural de la institución profesional," *Revista del Centro de Estudios Educativos* 8:3 (1978), pp. 137-162.

4. See Carr-Saunders and Wilson, *The Professions*, p. 307. Millerson notes that professions in Britain originally were closely tied to the church. "Anyone seeking entrance to, or promotion in, these occupations (physicians, lawyers, secretaries, surveyors, architects, teachers, and diplomats) automatically took holy orders, or minor orders." The last profession to secularize was university teaching, owing to strong ecclesiastic influence in higher education. See Millerson, *The Qualifying Associations*, pp. 16-17.

5. In a baseline empirical analysis of professional employment in Mexico, Adrián Lajous Vargas found that 21.43 percent of professionals in the service sector worked in government in 1967. See his *Aspectos de la educación superior y el empleo de profesionistas en México 1959-1967*, licenciate thesis, Escuela Nacional de Economía, 1967, p. 89. By 1970, the figure had risen to more than 50 percent (see chapter 5). Eliseo Mendoza Berrueto, while Subsecretary of Higher Education and Scientific Research of the Secretariat of Public Education, predicted that the number of professionals would increase from 700 thousand in 1981 to about 2 million in 1990. *Unomásuno*, June 11, 1981.

6. Even in Britain and the United States, Freidson warns against viewing professions "as collectivities of fully autonomous highly prestigious, individual entrepreneurs who can essentially do what they please . . . . Such an incomplete conception is neither analytically coherent nor empirically salient, even as an ideal type, to most professions since the nineteenth century." See "The Changing Nature of Professional Control," *Annual Review of Sociology* 10 (1984), p. 18. For bureaucratic control, see Howard M. Vollmer and Donald L. Mills, eds., *Professionalization* (Englewood Cliffs, New Jersey: Prentice-Hall, 1966), especially the chapter by W. Richard Scott, "Professionals in Bureaucracy— Areas of Conflict," pp. 266-276. Also, Corinne Lathrop Gilb, *Hidden Hierarchies: The Professions and Government* (New York: Harper & Row, 1966); and A. G. Fielding and D. Portwood, "Professions and the State—Towards a Typology of Bureaucratic Professions," *Sociological Review* 28:1 (February 1980), pp. 23-53. Terence Johnson, in *Professions and Power*, introduced the concept of "heteronomy," which refers to the intermediation of the state to remove from both an occupation and its client the authority to determine the content and manner of practice.

7. For a general description of this phenomenon, see Immanuel Wallerstein, *The Modern World System* (New York: Academic Press, 1974). Professional development in much of the Third World has emanated from universities, associations, and standards of professionalism in the metropolitan powers. An illustrative study is Terence J. Johnson and Marjorie Caygill, *Community in the Making: Aspects of Britain's Role in the Development of Professional Education in the Commonwealth* (London: University of London, Institute of Commonwealth Studies, 1972).

8. Larson, *The Rise of Professionalism*, p. 246; Millerson, *The Qualifying Associations*, pp. 246–258.

9. Mexico, Secretaría de Educación Pública, *Ley de profesiones (reformas)* (Mexico City: Dirección General de Información, 1974).

10. In a comparative survey of 51 countries, Donald Treiman finds that "there is a high agreement throughout the world regarding the relative prestige of occupations . . . (P)eople in all walks of life, rich and poor, educated and ignorant, urban and rural, male and female, view the prestige hierarchy in the same way." See Treiman, *Occupational Prestige in Comparative Perspective* (New York: Academic Press, 1977), pp. 96–97. The precursor to his work in the United States is Peter M. Blau and Otis Dudley Duncan, *The American Occupational Structure* (New York: John Wiley, 1967).

11. Only one study apparently has been conducted of occupational prestige in Mexico. See S. Jeffrey K. Wilkerson, "Occupational Prestige in Mexico as Perceived by College Students," *Human Mosaic* 2 (Fall 1967), pp. 56–64. Comparing these limited data with Treiman's scale indicates that occupations with prestige scores lower than the international average are military officer, soldier, and clergyman (because of the stigma placed on them by revolutionary folklore), congressman (for ineffectualness), and policeman (for abuse of power, and/or corruption). Fields with above-average prestige are school teacher (responsible for propagating nationalism), postman, road and factory worker (with relatively high income for low skills). See also, María Luisa Rodríguez Sala de Gómezgil, *El científico en México: su imagen entre los estudiantes de enseñanza media* (Mexico City: Universidad Nacional Autónoma de México, 1977).

12. Fourteen of sixteen respondents to this question placed medicine first (10) or second (4), manifesting a high degree of consensus on medicine's leading status position in Mexican society. Eleven placed agronomy last (6) or next to last (5), which at least shows the relatively low opinion that these urban-based respondents had of agronomy. Only economics and agronomy received no first place votes, even by members of these fields.

13. While doctors, economists, petroleum engineers, and agronomists came to similar rankings for each of the professions (their own included), they did not agree on law, which was "all over the map." Doctors and petroleum engineers placed law third on the list, which is the same as for the average. The economists placed it first, and the agronomists last. The implication is that the prestige of law is in flux.

14. Philip R. C. Elliott, *The Sociology of the Professions* (London: Macmillan, 1972).

15. For Talcott Parsons, "professional men are neither 'capitalists' nor 'workers' nor are they typically governmental administrators or bureaucrats." Bernard Barber's attributes of professional behavior are (a) generalized knowledge, (b) primary orientation to community rather than individual interest, (c) a code of ethics internalized partially through voluntary associations, and (d) pursuit of rewards which primarily symbolize work achievement as ends in themselves. Harold Wilensky refers to exclusive jurisdiction, autonomy, specialized training, and a professional association. He considers accounting, architecture, civil engineering, dentistry, law, and medicine as established in the United States; nursing and social work as in

process; city planning and hospital administration as new; and funeral direction as doubtful. See Parsons, "Professions," p. 539; Barber, "Some Problems in the Sociology of Professions," *Daedalus* 92:4 (Fall 1963), pp. 669–688; and Wilensky, "The Professionalization of Everyone?" *The American Journal of Sociology* 70:2 (September 1964), pp. 137–158. Summary analysis of these early functional analyses are prevalent in the literature. See, for example, Morris L. Cogan, "Toward the Definition of a Profession," *Harvard Educational Review* 23 (Winter 1953), pp. 33–50; Robert Gerald Storey, *Professional Leadership* (Pasadena, California: Castle Press, 1958); and Archie Kleingartner, *Professionalism and Salaried Worker Organization* (Madison, Wisconsin: Industrial Relations Research Institute, 1967).

16. Gabriel Gyarmati K., "The Doctrine of the Professions: Basis of a Power Structure," *International Social Science Journal* 27:4 (1975), p. 631.

17. Larson, *The Rise of Professionalsim*; Ivan Illich, et al, *The Disabling Professions* (London: Marion Boyers and Burns and MacEachern, 1977); Terence J. Johnson, "What is to be Known? The Structural Determination of Social Class," *Economy and Society* 6:2 (May 1977), pp. 194–233; and Ronald Frankenberg, "Allopathic Medicine, Profession, and Capitalist Ideology in India," *Social Science and Medicine* 15A:2 (1981), pp. 115–125.

Paul Boreham, Alex Pemberton, and Paul Wilson clearly typify this critical school by arguing that Australian society "is founded on unequal relationships between powerful and powerless groups or classes . . . (T)he powerful employ a wide range of 'technologies of consent' (in mass media and the educational system) to ensure their moral, cultural, and political hegemony over society," These authors allude to what they call professionals' "monopoly over knowledge" which, backed by the professional associations, has created a mystique in Australian society. See the edited volume, *The Professions in Australia: A Critical Appraisal* (St. Lucia, Queensland: University of Queensland Press, 1976), pp. 1–12.

18. Douglas Klegon, "The Sociology of Professions: An Emerging Perspective," *Sociology of Work and Occupations* 5:3 (August 1978), p. 269.

19. The concepts of "technicality" and "indeterminacy" were applied to professional knowledge by H. Jamous and B. Pellaille. The former pertains to that "portion of the means of production entirely susceptible to codification in terms of public rules, procedures, or techniques." The latter is a "variety of tacit or private knowledge that . . . cannot be made wholly explicit (and is) not transmissible by means of public and formal methods." According to these authors, this mysterious and indeterminate characteristic of professional expertise is one factor engendering professionals with prestige and power. See their "Professions or Self-Perpetuating System? Changes in the French University-Hospital System," in J. A. Jackson, ed., *Professions and Professionalization* (Cambridge: Cambridge University Press, 1970), pp. 109–152.

20. Randall Collins, *The Credential Society: An Historical Sociology of Education and Stratification* (New York: Academic Press, 1979).

21. Collins, *The Credential Society*, pp. 171–173.

22. Herbert Jacob, *German Administration since Bismarck: Central Authority versus Local Autonomy* (New Haven: Yale University Press, 1963), p. 200.

23. Jacob, *German Administration*, p. 201.

24. Dietrich Rueschemeyer, *Lawyers and their Society: A Comparative Study of the Legal Profession in Germany and in the United States* (Cambridge: Harvard University Press, 1973), p. 185. In justifying his comparative approach, he writes: "Among modern societies, England and the United States developed the most clear-cut forms of professional autonomy, and it is no accident that the corresponding theoretical model was developed by English and American social scientists. To generalize the model to professional work in all modern societies would be an act of intellectual parochialism" (p. 15).

25. Anthony J. LaVopa, *Prussian School Teachers: Profession and Office, 1763-1848* (Chapel Hill: University of North Carolina Press, 1980), p. 161. LaVopa does not worry himself with formal hypotheses. However, his conclusions on the nature of the teachers' work environment, as a "unique interstice between popular, largely rural culture and academic culture, between resistant communities and a meddling state bureaucracy," adds substance to Collins' notion of professional culture.

26. Collins, *The Credential Society*, p. 161. In France, Anne Steven comments on the powerful mix of elite training and bureaucratic position. The "success of the strategies of the *corps* as they have adapted themselves to new situations, giving priority to their own survival and the furtherance of their *corps* interest, has had its part to play in the acceptance by society of the *grands corps'* own image of themselves. The place occupied by . . . members of the *grands corps* in the direction of public and private enterprises . . . clearly illustrates the extent to which membership of the higher civil service, and particularly of a *grand corps,* is regarded as proof of an individual's capacity for the exercise of important responsibilities in the economic sphere, a capacity based both on his abilities and on the nature of his professional activites." See "The Higher Civil Service and Economic Policy-Making," in Philip G. Cerny and Martin A. Schain, eds., *French Politics and Public Policy* (New York: St. Martin's Press, 1980), pp. 84-85.

27. See Terence D. Murphy, "The French Medical Profession's Perception of its Social Function between 1776 and 1830," *Medical History* 23:3 (July 1979), pp. 259-278. During the French Revolution liberals attacked doctors' institutional and professional prestige, but the doctors were able to maintain their position because of the state's need for their attention to the wounded in the revolutionary wars.

28. Collins, pp. 141, 148.

29. D. M. Gvishian, S. R. Mikulinsky, and S. A. Kugel, *The Scientific Intelligentsia in the USSR* (Moscow: Progress Publishers, 1976), p. 137.

30. Richard Garfield, "Nursing, Health Care and Professionalism in Cuba," *Social Sciences and Medicine* 15A:1 (January 1981), p. 72 (emphasis in the original). See also, Mark Field, "Taming a Profession: Early Phases of Soviet Socialized Medicine," *Bulletin of the New York Academy of Medicine* 48 (1972).

31. Garfield, pp. 63–72.

32. Prominent writings on Latin American state systems are Philippe C. Schmitter, "Paths to Political Development in Latin America," in Douglas A. Chalmers, ed., *Changing Latin America* (New York: Academy of Political Science, 1972), pp. 83–109; and Alfred C. Stepan, *The State and Society,* pp. 3–45.

33. The contending hypothesis is postulated in Claudio Véliz, *The Centralist Tradition of Latin America* (Princeton: Princeton University Press, 1979).

34. Philippe C. Schmitter, "Still the Century of Corporatism?" in Fredrick B. Pike and Thomas Stritch, eds., *The New Corporatism: Social-Political Structures in the Iberian World* (Notre Dame: University of Notre Dame Press, 1974), pp. 93–94. See also, Howard J. Wiarda, "Toward a Framework for the Study of Political Change in the Iberic-Latin Tradition: The Corporative Model," *World Politics* 25:2 (January 1973), 206–235.

35. See the various interpretations in Lawrence E. Koslow and Stephen P. Mumme, "The Evolution of the Mexican Political System: A Paradigmatic Analysis," in Koslow, ed., *The Future of Mexico* (Tempe: Arizona State University, 1977), pp. 47–98; and Carolyn Needleman and Martin Needleman, "Who Rules Mexico? A Critique of some Current Views on the Mexican Political Process," *Journal of Politics* 31:4 (November 1969), pp. 1011–1034.

36. Pablo González Casanova, "México: el desarrollo más probable," in González Casanova and Enrique Florescano, eds., *México hoy* (Mexico City: Siglo XXI, 1979), pp. 405–419.

37. For a discussion of the effects of timing on other developmental processes, see David Collier, "Timing of Economic Growth and Regime Characteristics in Latin America," *Comparative Politics* 7:3 (April 1975), pp. 331–359.

38. See Merilee S. Grindle, ed., *Policy Implementation in the Third World* (Princeton: Princeton University Press, 1980). For professional competition in bureaucracy, see Peter S. Cleaves, *Bureaucratic Politics and Administration in Chile* (Berkeley: University of California Press, 1974); also, Oscar Oszlak, "Notas críticas para una teoría de la burocracia estatal," *Revista Mexicana de Sociología* 60:30 (July-September 1978), pp. 881–926.

39. Suleiman, in *Politics, Power, and Bureaucracy in France*, p. 381, notes that it is a "truism that a member of a group, or class, or profession does not necessarily represent his group occupying an independent position of power." In the past, Mexican professionals confirmed this rule, especially when appointed to positions outside their speciality. The question posed here pertains to the likely results when professionals occupy almost all key technical and administrative posts in a bureaucratic agency, and the agency itself is headed by a politician/professional in the same field.

40. Many Mexican professionals, especially those trained abroad, fail to recognize the unique trajectory of professionalism in Mexico, and are excessively normative or cynical in their judgments concerning the quality and contributions of these fields in their country.

41. In the nineteeth and early twentieth centuries, French, German, and Spanish writings were widely read by Mexican law students, who received eclectic philosophical training. After the Revolution, however, discussions of the social uses of the law revolved mainly around the clauses of the 1917 Constitution and its derivative legislation. See the thorough analysis of Roderic Ai Camp, *La formación de un gobernante: la socialización de los líderes políticos en el México posrevolucionario* (Mexico City: Siglo XXI, 1981), pp. 104–128.

42. See Daniel López Acuña, "Salud y seguirdad social: problemas recientes y alternativas," and Arturo Warman, "El problema del campo," in González Casanova and Florescano, eds., *México hoy,* pp. 177–219 and 108–120.

43. See the two censuses of human resources in the state sector: Mexico, *Censo de recursos humanos del sector público federal: administración central 1975,* and *Administración decentralizada y de participación estatal mayoritaria 1975,* both (Mexico City: Comisión de Recursos Humanos del Gobierno Federal, 1976).

CHAPTER TWO: NATIONALISM IN MEXICAN PROFESSIONS

1. See Toribio Esquivel Obregón, *Apuntes para la historia del derecho en México* (Mexico City: Publicidad y Ediciones, 1943); Lucio A. Cabrera, "History of the Mexican Judiciary," *Miami Law Quarterly* 439 (Summer 1957); and, for legal developments in the period 1968 to 1977, the two-volume issue of *Jurídica* 10 (July 1978), published by Iberoamerican University.

2. George W. Grayson, *The Politics of Mexican Oil* (Pittsburgh: University of Pittsburgh Press, 1980), pp. 3–18; also, Eduardo Cervera, "La enseñanza de la ingeniería petrolera en la Universidad Nacional Autónoma de México," unpublished paper presented to the Panamerican Congress of Petroleum Engineering, Winter 1979.

3. Antonio J. Bermúdez, *The Mexican National Petroleum Industry* (Stanford: Institute of Hispanic American and Luso-Brazilian Studies, Stanford University, 1963), pp. 24–27. Another large U.S. concern, the Mexican Gulf Oil Company (Gulf Oil), was not expropriated in 1938, but was purchased in 1951. See also Lorenzo Meyer, *Mexico and the United States in the Oil Controversy* (Austin: University of Texas Press, 1977).

4. Interview No. 31.

5. "IMP Aims at Making the Nation Leader in Petrochemicals," *R&D Mexico* 2:1 (October 1981), pp. 11–17.

6. Interview No. 29.

7. Interview No. 27.

8. Compare the hopeful treatment of the agrarian production unit in Eyler N. Simpson, *The Ejido: Mexico's Way Out* (Chapel Hill: University of North Carolina Press, 1937), with the much later, more pessimistic treatment in P. Lamartine Yates, *Mexico's Agricultural Dilemma* (Tucson: University of Arizona Press, 1981).

9. Interview No. 23.

10. See Adolfo Orive Alba, *La irrigación en México* (Mexico City: Editorial Grijalva, 1970); Thomas G. Sanders, "Population Growth and Resource Management: Planning Mexico's Water Supply," *American Universities Field Staff Reports,* North American Series 2:3 (1974), pp. 1–16; Emilio López Zamora, *El agua, la tierra, los hombres de México* (Mexico City: Fondo de Cultural Económica, 1977); and Miguel S. Wionczek, "La aportación de la política hidráulica entre 1925 y 1970 a la actual crisis agrícola mexicana," *Comercio Exterior* 32:4 (April 1982), pp. 394–409.

11. See Ramón Fernández y Fernández, *Chapingo hace cincuenta años* (Chapingo: Colegio de Postgraduados, Escuela Nacional de Agricultura, 1976).

12. Prior to the *campesinistas*, the nationalist wing of the agronomy profession, identified with Jesús Uribe Ruiz, rejected contamination by U.S. agricultural approaches. The *campesinistas* have various academic spokespersons in Mexico, inspired by the previous writings of both non-Marxists and Marxists (Schultz, Kautsky, Wolf, Chayanov, Lenin). See, for example, David Barkin, *Desarrollo regional y reorganización campesina* (Mexico City: Nueva Imagen, 1978); Armando Bartra, "Colectivización o proletarización: el caso del Plan Chontalpa," *Cuadernos Agrarios* 1:4 (October-December 1976), pp. 56–111; Gustavo Esteva, "¿Y si los campesinos existen?" *Comercio Exterior* 28:6 (June 1978), pp. 699–732: Abraham Iszaevich, *Modernización campesina* (Mexico City: Editorial Edicol, 1980); Arturo Warman, *Y venimos a contradecir* (Mexico City: Ediciones Casa Chata, 1976). For a thorough analysis of the implications of agricultural modernization for rural laborers, including an examination of the Mexican case, see David Goodman and Michael Redclift, *From Peasant to Proletarian: Capitalist Development and Agrarian Transitions* (Oxford: Basil Blackwell, 1981).

13. The fiscal policies later dubbed "stabilizing development" were based on tax incentives for industry, price stability, foreign investment, indirect taxation, free convertibility of the peso, a fixed exchange rate, and, as imports grew, foreign borrowing. The result was a growth rate of 6 to 7 percent per year during the 1960s. See Clark W. Reynolds, "Why Mexico's 'Stabilizing Development' was Actually Destabilizing (with some Implications for the Future)," Council on Foreign Relations, Current Issues Review Group on U.S.-Mexican Relations, April 5, 1977.

14. The key institutions in the Mexican financial sector are Hacienda y Crédito Público (Treasury), Programación y Presupuesto (Planning and Budgeting), NAFINSA (the development bank), SEPAFIN, the Banco de México (central bank), and IMCE (see List of Acronyms).

15. Víctor Urquidi later became president of the Colegio de México; Octaviano Campos Salas, Secretary of Industry and Commerce; Raúl Salinas, Secretary of Industry: Raúl Ortiz Mena, Subsecretary of the Presidency; and Alfonso Pulido Islas, advisor to the Secretariat of the Treasury. See Roderic Ai Camp, *Mexican Political Biographies 1935–1975* (Tucson: University of Arizona Press, 1976).

16. See Roderic Ai Camp, "The National School of Economics and Public Life in Mexico," *Latin American Research Review* 10:3 (Fall 1975), pp. 137–153. Also, Ma. Teresa Fernández Lozano, "La formación de economistas en México," *El Economista Mexicano* 12:3 (May-June 1978), pp. 21–26.

17. For examples of these approaches, see Horacio Flores de la Peña, *Los obstáculos al desarrollo económico (el desequilibrio fundamental)*, dissertation, Escuela Nacional de Economía, National Autonomous University of Mexico, 1955; Carlos Tello, *La política económica en México 1970–1976* (Mexico City: Siglo XXI, 1979); José Ayala, José Blanco, Rolando Cordera, Guillermo Knockenhauer, and Armando Labra, "La crisis económico: evolución y perspectivas," in González Casanova and Florescano, eds., *México hoy*, pp. 19–96; and the journal published by the Centro de Investigación y Docencia Económicas, *Economía mexicana: análisis y perspectivas*. The 1982 bank

nationalization was planned and executed by persons generally associated with the nationalist group.

18. A book characteristic of this school is Raymond Vernon, *The Dilemma of Mexico's Development* (Cambridge: Harvard University Press, 1963).

19. Interview No. 7.

20. Interview Nos. 9 and 10.

21. See Fernando H. Cardoso, "La originalidad de la copia: la CEPAL y la idea de desarrollo," in René Villarreal, ed., *Economía internacional II. Teorías de imperialismo, la dependencia y su evidencia histórica* (Mexico City: Fondo de Cultura Económica, 1979), pp. 175–215.

22. Interview No. 10

23. The SDN (defense secretariat) health service, formerly called the Dirección de Pensiones Militares, is now the Instituto de Seguridad Social para las Fuerzas Armadas Mexicanas.

24. For analyses of traditional medicine in Mexico, see Carlos Viesca Treviño, ed., *Estudios sobre la etnobotánica y antropología médica*, 3 vols. (Mexico City: Centro de Estudios Económicos y Sociales del Tercer Mundo, 1976, 1977, 1978); Axel Ramírez, *Bibliografía comentada de la medicina tradicional mexicana (1900-1978)* (Mexico City: Instituto Mexicano para el Estudio de las Plantas Medicinales, 1978); Joseph Simoni and Richard A. Ball, "The Mexican Medical Huckster," *Sociology of Work and Occupations* 4:3 (August 1977), pp. 343–365; Isabel T. Kelly, *Folk Practices in North Mexico* (Austin: University of Texas Press, 1965); Horacio Fabrega, Jr., *Disease and Social Behavior: An Interdisciplinary Perspective* (Cambridge: MIT Press, 1974). Homeopathy, which has a following in Mexico, does not share the pharmaceutical emphasis of the biological approach. Homeopathy derives from the work of the German physician Samuel Christian Hahnemann (1755-1843), who rejected the prevalent remedies of the time (bleeding and blistering). Homeopathy's basic law is "let likes be cured by likes," which suggests that disease can be cured by drugs that produce in a healthy person the symptoms found in those who are ill. The law of infinitesimals indicates that the smaller the dose, the more effective the drug in stimulating the vital forces. See Martin Kaufman, *Homeopathy in America* (Baltimore: Johns Hopkins University Press, 1971). In Mexico, homeopaths are trained mainly at the Escuela Nacional de Medicina Homeopática of the IPN and the Escuela Libre de Homeopatía, founded in 1912, and they number about two thousand practitioners. See the interview with Dr. José Luis Huerta, "La homeopatía, práctica médica transformada en arte," *Unomásuno*, July 1, 1981; and *Unomásuno*, July 10, 1981. The homeopaths achieved a good measure of political power during the government of Emilio Portes Gil and Luis Echeverría because they were physicians for the presidential family (and, therefore, also a good portion of the cabinet). The major medical institutions, such as the IMSS and ISSSTE, decline to employ homeopaths, but their doctors will refer patients to homeopaths when biological approaches fail to provide a cure.

25. For background on the Mexican medical profession, see Ignacio Chávez, *México en la cultura médica* (Mexico City: El Colegio Nacional, 1947); Gordon Schendel, et al., *Medicine in Mexico* (Austin: University of Texas Press, 1968); CONACYT, *La ciencia y la tecnología en el sector medicina y salud: diagnóstico y política* (Mexico City: Consejo Nacional de Ciencia y Tecnología,

1976); and Tarsicio Ocampo V., ed., *México: socialización de la medicina 1965* (Cuernavaca: Centro Intercultural de Documentación CIDOC, Dossier No. 18, 1968). The National Academy of Medicine is compiling a history of Mexican medicine to be published in several volumes.

26. Interview No. 12.

27. For an analysis of the Mexican health system, see Daniel López Acuña, "Salud y seguridad social: problemas recientes y alternativas," in González Casanova y Florescano, eds., *México hoy*, pp. 177-219. Viviane Márquez is preparing a major book on public health policy in Mexico.

28. Interview No. 16.

29. Interview No. 14.

30. Interview No. 4.

31. Interview No. 16.

32. Census data from public sector enterprises are not broken down by speciality so it is not possible to ascertain how many doctors hold alternative employment. The results of the most recent survey provided the following figures for *all* employees in several state medical institutions:

Institution	Total Employees	With Two Jobs	Second Job in:			
			Central Agency	Decent. Agency	Private	Other
SSA	58,250	6,920	2,223	2,126	1,136	1,435
IMSS	93,166	9,042	2,906	1,588	2,836	1,712
Children's Hospital	2,093	365	137	118	55	55
Heart Institute	1,139	185	26	73	36	50
Cancer Institute	109	25	13	7	—	5
Totals	154,757	16,537	5,305	3,912	4,063	3,257

These figures would indicate that only 10.68 percent of public employees in these institutes had second jobs. Since the information is based on the subjects' responses to a questionnaire, it is likely that the figures are underestimates. See Mexico, *Censo de recursos humanos del sector público federal: administración central*, pp. 130-131; and *Administración decentralizada*, pp. 246-266.

33. Interview No. 11.

34. Interview No. 14.

35. Those who feel that the peasantry is destined to disappear include modernizing theorists (such as Walt Rostow, Gino Germani, and, in Mexico, Ramón Fernández y Fernández) and Marxist thinkers (V. Lenin and, in Mexico, Roger Bartra and Luisa Paré). I am grateful to Abraham Iszaevich for this observation.

36. Fields other than those described here have experienced this division; for example, architecture. Narciso Bassols, during his term as Secretary of Education (1931-1934), encouraged the development of what came to be called "Mexican

architecture" at the National University. Major figures were Juan O'Gorman, Enrique Yáñez, Enrique Guerrero, and Raúl Cacho. Their approach emphasized austere lines and economical building materials. The cosmopolitan architects, who looked mainly to Europe for inspiration, were José Villagrán García, Pablo Flores, and Luis Legorreta. By the mid-1940s "Mexican architecture" had lost impetus and the international current predominated.

CHAPTER THREE: THE ROLE OF UNIVERSITY EDUCATION IN PROFESSIONAL TRAINING

1. See Magali Sarfatti Larson, *The Rise of Professionalism* (Berkeley: University of California Press, 1977), pp. 3-4, 136, 144. For comments on professional education, see Ronald Gross and Paul Osterman, eds., *The New Professionals* (New York: Simon and Schuster, 1972); and Everett C. Hughes, et al., *Education for the Professions of Medicine, Law, Theology, and Social Welfare* (New York: McGraw-Hill, 1973).

2. The consequence for the Latin American university is dubbed "massification." See Jaime Rodríguez Forero, "El concepto de masificación: su importancia y perspectivas para el análisis de la educación superior," in *Fichas* (Buenos Aires: UNESCO, CEPAL, PNUD, 1978), pp. 1-49; Alistair Hennesy, "Students in the Latin American University," in Joseph Maier and Richard W. Weatherhead, eds., *The Latin American University* (Albuquerque: University of New Mexico Press, 1979), pp. 147-184; Judith K. Barr and Charles E. Barr, "The Structure of the Dental Profession and the Use of Auxiliaries in Latin America," *Social Science and Medicine* 14A:2 (March 1980), 107-111; and, for Mexico, Alfredo Tecla Jiménez, *Universidad, burguesía y proletariado* (Mexico City: Cultura Popular, 1976).

While more prominent in Latin America, burgeoning university enrollments are a worldwide phenomenon. From 1970 to 1976, the number of students in university, professional, and teachers colleges increased by 54 percent worldwide (24.4 to 37.6 million) and 150 percent in Latin America (1.4 to 3.5 million); United Nations, *Statistical Yearbook* (New York: United Nations, 1972, 1979). Many advanced industrialized countries suffer from the problem of devalued university degrees. For discussion of the United States, Britain, and Canada, respectively, see Richard B. Freeman, *The Over-Educated American* (New York: Academic Press, 1976), pp. 17-21; Richard Berthoud, *Unemployed Professionals and Executives* (London: Policy Studies Institute, No. 582, May, 1979), p. 2; and L.W.C.S. Barnes, "The Changing Stance of the Professional Employee," *Research Series* 29 (1975), Industrial Relations Centre, Queen's University at Kingston, pp. 20-22.

3. Compare with the scheme in Larissa Lomnitz, "Conflict and Mediation in a Latin American University," *Journal of Inter-American Studies and World Affairs* 19:3 (August 1977), pp. 315-338.

4. See Universidad Nacional Autónoma de México, *Anuario Estadístico 1977* (Mexico City: Secretario General de Servicios Auxiliares, 1978), pp. 192-196. Income distribution figures for Mexico in the same year are available from Enrique Hernández Laos and Jorge Córdova Chávez, "Estructuras de la distribución del ingreso en México," *Comercio Exterior* 29:5 (May 1979), pp. 505-520. The characteristics of Mexico's income pyramid are such, however, that

families earning 8000 pesos in 1977 were in the ninth highest decile. The UNAM and Hernández-Córdova data do not divide the respective populations in the same way; that notwithstanding, it is possible to extrapolate that 8.6 percent of UNAM students were in the fourth decile (averaging 2004 pesos/month) or below, 42.2 percent were in the seventh decile (averaging 4398 pesos/month) or below, and 64.1 percent were in the eighth decile (5779 pesos/month) or below. Prior to "massification," UNAM students generally came from the top five percent of the income pyramid.

5. Daniel C. Levy argues that the Mexican government's political priorities in higher education are (a) to maintain the current social order, (b) to respond to immediate demands, and (c) to implement policy options. All presidential regimes subscribe to (a), but only the Echeverría government seemed interested in (c). See his *University and Government in Mexico: Autonomy in an Authoritarian System* (New York: Praeger, 1980); also, Fernando Pérez Correa, "La universidad: contradicciones y perspectivas," *Foro Internacional 55* 14:3 (January-March 1974), pp. 375-401.

6. In 1979 the UNAM absorbed 42 percent of public expenditures for higher education. See Levy, *University and Government*, pp. 108-111. Levy's interpretation of the budgetary and entrance predicament is more benign than the one presented here. First, he notes that at the time of his research the government's priority disciplines for national development were agriculture, natural sciences, engineering, and medical sciences, with humanities and the social sciences at the bottom (pp. 121-125). However, funding levels bore little relationship to this list. Second, he argues that student pressure can force high enrollment, and that students, through their numbers, can govern budgetary allocations. These facts are supportive, Levy believes, of university autonomy and student freedom. He does not deal specifically with the issue of low academic quality.

7. See Larissa Lomnitz, "The Exercise of Power in a Latin American University," paper prepared for the Burg Wartenstein Symposium No. 84, Werner-Gren Foundation, New York, July, 1980.

8. For 1966, see Unión de Universidades de América Latina, *Censo Universitario Latinoamerico 1966-1969* (Mexico City: UDUAL, 1971), p. 715; for 1979, see Universidad Nacional Autónoma de México, *Anuario Estadístico 1979* (Mexico City: Secretaría General Administrativa, 1980), p. 169, 296.

9. Unpublished statistics, Department of Petroleum Engineering, UNAM, 1981.

10. Interview No. 37.

11. Larissa Lomnitz speaks of "fighting gangs" in "Conflict and Mediation in a Latin American University," pp. 330-331. See also C. C. Guitián, *Las porras: estudio de caso de un grupo de presión universitaria*, licenciate thesis, Escuela de Ciencias Sociales y Políticas, Universidad Nacional Autónoma de México, 1975.

12. See Asociación Mexicana de Educación Agrícola Superior, *Información General* (Mexico City: AMEAS, 1980). The ANUIES figure is 38 undergraduate programs for 1980.

13. See Bernardo Sepúlveda, ed., *Seminario sobre Educación Superior: Ponencias* (Mexico City: El Colegio Nacional, 1979), especially pp. 127–159, which reports fifty-five medical schools.

14. Interview No. 5.

15. See Roderic Ai Camp, *The Role of the "Técnico" in Policy-Making in Mexico: A Comparative Study of Developing Bureaucracy*, Ph.D. dissertation, University of Arizona, 1970, p. 44.

16. See Cynthia Vice Acosta, "CONACYT: 26,000 Study Grants," *R&D Mexico* 2:1 (October 1981), pp. 47–48.

17. Interview No. 5.

18. See Nigel Brooke, "Actitudes de los empleadores mexicanos respecto a la educación: ¿un test de la teoría del capital humano?" *Revista del Centro de Estudios Educativos* 8:4 (1978), pp. 109–132, in which he discovers through interviews that employers look to the quality and length of formal training as indicators of how easily new employees can be trained and socialized.

19. Interviews Nos. 4, 12.

20. Although in 1970 there was one doctor for each 474 inhabitants in the Federal District, the figures for Zacatecas were one for each 4344, and in Chiapas one for each 4601. See CONACYT, *La ciencia y la technología en el sector medicina y salud: diagnóstico y política* (Mexico City: Consejo Nacional de Ciencia y Tecnología, 1976), p. 45.

21. Interview No. 8.

22. Interview No. 22. Personal contacts also play a part in obtaining these positions, although the examination cannot be avoided altogether. See Larissa Lomnitz, Leticia Mayer, and Marta W. Rees, "Recruiting Technical Elites: Mexico's Veterinarians," mimeograph, Institute of Applied Statistics, Universidad Nacional Autónoma de Mexico, 1982. In agencies such as PEMEX and CFE, the union intervenes in the process, distorting entrance standards. When CFE officials wish to control quality through entrance examinations (for example, to hire engineers to build and run nuclear power plants), they must negotiate a special dispensation from the union, which resists infringements on its autonomy. Most professionals pay the union directly to obtain their positions.

23. Interview No. 19.

CHAPTER FOUR: THE ORGANIZED PROMOTION OF PROFESSIONAL INTERESTS

1. Geoffrey Millerson, *The Qualifying Associations* (London: Routledge and Kegan Paul, 1964), pp. 28–32.

2. See also, Magali Sarfatti Larson, *The Rise of Professionalism* (Berkeley: University of California Press, 1977), p. 15.

3. See Wilbert E. Moore, *The Professions: Roles and Rules* (New York: Russell Sage Foundation, 1970), pp. 157–173.

4. Maurie Haug, "The Sociological Approach to Self-Regulation," in Roger D. Blair and Stephen Rubin, eds., *Regulating the Professions* (Lexington, Massachusetts: D. C. Heath & Company, 1980), p. 74. Similarly, Arlene Kaplan Daniels argues that the "history of professions and professionalism does not

really seem to support the contention that professional autonomy contributes to high standards of professional service. Instead, we find the more powerful the profession, the more serious the charges of laxness in concern for public service and zealousness in promoting the individual interests of the practitioners," See "How Free Should Professions Be?" in Eliot Freidson, ed., *The Professions and Their Prospects* (Beverly Hills, California: Sage Publications, 1973), p. 55. Professional associations are reluctant to release data on registered cases of incompetence, ethical breaches, censure, and disbarment. An exception is the Institute of Chartered Accountants in England and Wales, whose disciplinary actions from 1949 to 1962 were 10 expulsions, 11 suspensions, 77 reprimands, and 25 admonishments, altogether representing .02 percent of practicing members each year. See Millerson, *Qualifying Associations*, pp. 176-177.

5. See Richard W. Judy, "The Economists," and Donald D. Barry and Harold J. Berman, "The Jurists," in H. Gordon Skilling and Franklin Griffiths, eds., *Interest Groups in Soviet Politics* (Princeton: Princeton University Press, 1971), pp. 209-251, 291-333. Nicholas Lambert describes the means used by the Soviet state, in the 1928-1935 period, to undermine professionals' corporate loyalties and redirect them to the goals of the Revolution. After the initial phase, managers of state enterprises were able to achieve a measure of professional autonomy by determing how they would meet production goals. See Lambert, *The Technical Intelligentsia and the Soviet State* (New York: Holmes and Meier, 1979). L.G. Churchwood writes that professional associations "representing particular professional groups within the intelligentsia, are relatively unimportant in the Soviet Union . . . . The existing professional organizations fall into two broad groups—those organized directly by the Party in order to increase its ideological control over strategic sections of the intelligentsia such as writers . . . and organizations of particular segments of intellectuals where a professional organization is almost a condition of . . . participation in international conferences . . . . Associations like the above do not have any real life." Churchwood, *The Soviet Intelligentsia* (London: Routledge and Kegan Paul, 1973), pp. 63-64.

6. Ernest Simmons, "The Writers," in Skilling and Griffiths, *Interest Groups in Soviet Politics*, p. 253. For a well-documented but dated perspective, see Nicolas DeWitt, *Education and Professional Employment in the U.S.S.R.* (Washington: U.S. Government Printing Office, 1961). A Soviet analysis states that science is being "institutionalized" into a mass profession, "while the planning of research, the number of personnel, and the distribution of the scientific establishment is centralized." See D. M. Gvishian et al., *The Scientific Intelligentsia in the U.S.S.R.*, p. 39.

7. See David Collier and Ruth B. Collier, "Who Does What, to Whom, and How: Toward a Comparative Analysis of Latin America," in James M. Malloy, ed., *Authoritarianism and Corporatism in Latin America* (Pittsburgh: University of Pittsburgh Press, 1977), pp. 489-512.

8. In Nigeria, for example, traditional healers have been organized in regional professional associations at least since the nineteenth century. See D. D. O. Oyebola, "Professional Associations, Ethics and Discipline among Yoruba Traditional Healers of Nigeria," *Social Science and Medicine* 15B:2 (April 1981), pp. 87-92.

9. See Mexico, Secretaría de Educación Pública, *Ley de Profesiones (Reformas)* (Mexico City: Dirección General de Información, 1974).

10. Information gathered from the respective organizations by Araceli Marín.

11. A partial list of other professional associations in various fields is as follows: medicine—Asociación de Médicos Mexicanos, Asociación Mexicana de Ginecología y Obstetricia, Socieded Mexicana de Pediatría, Asociación Médica del ISSTE, Asociación Médica Diagnóstico Nacional, Asociación Médico-Quirúrgica, Colegio Nacional de Médicos Militares, Federación Mexicana de Asociaciones de Ginecología y Obstetricia, Fundación Mexicana de Cardiología, Asociación Mexicana de Facultades y Escuelas de Médicina, Asociación Mexicana de Gastroenterología, Sociedad Mexicana de Hematología, Academia Mexicana de Cirugía; engineering—Asociación de Ingenieros y Arquitectos de México, Asociación de Ingenieros Universitarios Mecánicos Elcctricistas, Asociación Mexicana de Ingenieros Mecánicos y Electricistas, Asociación Mexicana de Ingenieros Industriales, Colegio de Ingenieros Mécanicos y Electricistas, Colegio de Ingenieros y Arquitectos del Ejido de México, Instituto Mexicano de Ingenieros, Asociación de Ingenieros de Minas Metalúrgicas y Geólogos de México, Asociación de Facultades y Escuelas de Ingeniería, Colegio Nacional de Ingenieros y Arquitectos de México, Asociación de Técnicos, Ingenieros y Profesionales; law—Asociación Nacional de Abogados de Empresas; agriculture—Asociación Nacional de Egresados de la Escuela Superior de Agricultura, Confederación Agronómica Mexicana; petroleum cngineering—Colegio de Ingenieros Químicos y Químicos de la Ciudad de México, Instituto Mexicano de Ingenieros Químicos; economists—Sociedad Mexicana de Planificación, Economistas Precursores Universitarios; architecture—Colegio de Arquitectura de México; accounting—Colegio de Contadores Públicos de México, Instituto Mexicano de Contadores Públicos, Asociación Nacional de Contadores.

12. Interview No. 26.

13. Interview No. 36.

14. Interview No. 37.

15. Interview No. 20.

16. Interview No. 35.

17. Interview No. 37.

18. The meaning of *camarilla* is imprecise, and not all agree that the term is conceptually or empirically valid. Peter Smith calls *camarillas* "groups bound by loyalty to an individual leader . . . who is expected to award patronage in return for their support," in *Labyrinths of Power: Political Recruitment in Twentieth-Century Mexico* (Princeton: Princeton University Press, 1979), p. 50. Larissa Lomnitz prefers the notion of "networks." See "Horizontal and Vertical Relations and the Social Structure of Urban Mexico," *Latin American Research Review* 17:2 (1982), 51–74.

19. Interview No. 35.

20. The figure, of course, is a rough estimate. For a careful analysis of feminist inroads into the Mexican political elite, see Roderic Ai Camp, "Women and Political Leadership in Mexico: A Comparative Study of Female and Male Political Elites," *Journal of Politics* 41:2 (May 1979), pp. 417–441. Camp finds

that from 1958 to 1979, an average of eleven women per three-year term of office held seats in the Chamber of Deputies.

21. Interview No. 19.

22. Interview No. 18.

23. Information for this section was derived from interviews with strike participants and from Tarsicio Ocampo V., ed., *México: socialización de la medicina* (Cuernavaca: Centro Intercultural de Documentación CIDOC, Dossier No. 18, 1968). It is important to note that, while the strike was an effort for doctors to exert greater control over their occupational affairs, its leaders made little effort to generate higher-level political demands. The most complete analysis of the doctors' movement is Evelyn P. Stevens, *Protest and Response in Mexico* (Cambridge: MIT Press, 1974), pp. 126–184.

24. Interview No. 16.

25. The Political Constitution abets this intention by governing unionization. Paragraph A of Article 123 covers private sector and para-state workers, and formally permits a large number of unions at the factory, industry, regional, and national levels. Paragraph B pertains to workers in the central government, and decrees that workers must belong to the one union designated to represent their interests in the bureaucratic unit. Since Paragraph A applies to IMSS and Paragraph B to SSA, a single union for doctors from both health entities (not to mention ISSSTE, PEMEX, and the others) would be "unconstitutional."

26. Interview No. 12.

27. See Viviane Márquez, "Estructura del sector público de la salud en México: problemas y perspectivas," paper presented to the Fifth Congress of Social Work, Mexico City, April 2–4, 1981.

28. In 1981, former UNAM rector Guillermo Soberón was asked to examine the advisability of unifying the health system. After several months of study, he reported, and President López Portillo confirmed, that it was "technically unfeasible." See *Unomásuno*, December 1, 1981, p. 1. A similar policy proposal was reviewed at the end of the Echeverría administration and likewise rejected. Israel, as a state-dominant system, presents certain parallels with Mexico. See Joseph Ben-David, "Professionals and Unions in Israel," in Eliot Freidson and Judith Lorber, eds., *Medical Men and their Work* (Chicago: Aldine Atherton, 1972), pp. 20–38.

29. For an excellent discussion of the petroleum union, see George W. Grayson, *The Politics of Mexican Oil* (Pittsburgh: University of Pittsburgh Press, 1980), pp. 81–102. A comparable union is attached to the Federal Electricity Commission. See Silvia Gómez Tagle, *Insurgencia y democracia en los sindicatos electricistas* (Mexico City: El Colegio de México, 1980), especially pp. 132–138. These books, however, do not elaborate on the predicament of professional employees in the two unions.

30. Secretaría de Programación y Presupuesto, *La industria petrolera en México* (Mexico City: Coordinación General del Sistema Nacional de Información, 1979), pp. 377–378.

31. Interview No. 27.

32. Interview No. 7.

33. Interview No. 5.

34. Interview No. 8.

35. For a summary of these events, see *Información Sistemática* 5:51 (April 15, 1980), pp. 16-17. Mexico eventually applied for GATT membership in 1986.

36. See *Proceso* 5:237 (May 18, 1981), pp. 6-9.

CHAPTER FIVE: PROFESSIONS AND THE STATE

1. The notion of "professional project" comes from Magali Sarfatti Larson, *The Rise of Professionalism* (Berkeley: University of California Press, 1977), pp. 49-52.

2. Terence J. Johnson, *Professions and Power* (London: Macmillan, 1972), pp. 14-18, discusses the controversy between those who view bureaucratic power in the hands of professionals in a positive light and those who see it in a negative light. Professions in organization can be either a force for independence and rational thought or so narrowly specialized that they represent a bureaucratic threat to a free citizenry. Alvin W. Gouldner assigns labels implied by various authors to describe the "new class," which is composed of technical intelligentsia and intellectuals: (a) benign technocrats (Galbraith, Bell), (b) a Master Class (Bakunin), (c) an old class ally (Parsons), (d) servants of power (Chomsky, Zeitlin), or (e) a flawed universal class (Gouldner himself). See *The Future of Intellectuals and the Rise of the New Class* (New York: Continuum, 1979), p. 6-7.

3. In Mexico, Pablo Latapí is one of those most disquieted by the effect of professionalization on social inequality. See "Profesiones y sociedad," unpublished manuscript, Prospectiva Universitaria, 1982.

4. Important analyses of Mexican technocrats are: Guillermo Kelly, "Politics and Administration in Mexico: Recruitment and Promotion of the Politico-Administrative Class," *Technical Papers Series* (33), Institute of Latin American Studies, University of Texas at Austin, 1981; Roderic Ai Camp, "The Middle-Level Technocrat in Mexico," *Journal of Developing Areas* 6:4 (July 1972), pp. 571-582; Merilee S. Grindle, "Power, Expertise and the 'Tecnico': Suggestions from a Mexican Case Study," *Journal of Politics* 39:2 (May 1977), pp. 399-426; and Martin Harry Greenberg, *Bureaucracy and Development* (Lexington, Massachusetts: D. C. Heath and Company, 1970), pp. 99-130.

5. Lenard J. Cohen, "Partisans, Professionals, and Proletarians: Elite Change in Yugoslavia, 1952-1978," *Canadian Slavonic Papers* 21:4 (December 1979), pp. 446-478. Cohen's article is a contribution to the discussion of the dual-elite syndrome, consisting of technocrats and ideologues, in communist systems. The analogous phenomenon in Mexico involves competition and collaboration between those following a "political" and those following an "administrative" career path. See Peter H. Smith, *Labyrinths of Power: Political Recruitment in Twentieth-Century Mexico* (Princeton: Princeton University Press, 1979), pp. 146, 207-208; and, for the López Portillo administration, Roderic Ai Camp, "Political Recruitment and Change: Mexico in the 1970s," unpublished manuscript, Central College, Pella, Iowa, 1982.

6. Suleiman, *Politics, Power, and Bureaucracy in France* (Princeton: Princeton University Press, 1974), p. 382.

7. Grindle, "Power, Expertise and the 'Técnico'," pp. 414-416.

8. Grindle, p. 421.

9. Thomas A. Baylis, *The Technical Intelligentsia and the East German Elite: Legitimacy and Social Change in Mature Communism* (Berkeley: University of California Press, 1974), pp. 12–13.

10. Doctors vent their exasperation: "Has the doctor been important in health policy? I can say categorically not. As a doctor of the presidential family, yes, a doctor has political clout. But in institutionalized medicine, no . . . . Who are the doctors who have advanced in political influence? Are they the best trained? Or are they the ones with good connections with the politicians or the President? Naturally, the answer is the latter." (Interview No. 12)

11. Interview No. 15.

12. A full-time teacher and researcher in the profession expressed his sentiments: "Sometimes agronomists do render an opinion, and it is always consistent with the government's policies. As far as I can remember over the past thirty years, agronomists have only and always supported the government. But as for discussion, it just does not exist. There are no fights. All of Mexico is a paradise. ¡Vaya! This is a peaceful country." (Interview No. 19)

13. Interview No. 19.

14. Interview No. 8.

15. Interview No. 37.

16. See Clark W. Reynolds, *The Mexican Economy: Twentieth-Century Structure and Growth* (New Haven: Yale University Press, 1970), pp. 89–160.

17. For a capsule description of these two measures, see John J. Bailey, "Agrarian Reform in Mexico: The Quest for Self-Sufficiency," *Current History* 80:469 (November 1981), pp. 357–360.

18. The latter policy was called SAM. One agronomist interviewed had advocated for years that a SAM-like policy be adopted, and he and another agronomist were drafted into a legislative team made up of about a dozen persons, mainly economists and lawyers. In discussing his role, however, he cautioned: "You must remember that we did not intervene in SAM as a profession, but as politicians. We were a couple of (individuals) with social concerns. There was little debate within the profession over the measures." (Interview No. 26) Another agronomist preferred to count his blessings rather than complain: "Maybe it was some *licenciados* and not the agronomists who formulated the SAM policy . . . but that's OK. If *el señor Presidente* says we need the SAM for this and that reason, the situation suddenly improves . . . . You get the budget, the people, and the authority." (Interview No. 18)

19. Carlos Tello, a major protagonist in the bank nationalization, had maintained periodic contact with President López Portillo after his ouster as Secretary of Programming and Budgeting. He and others began planning for the September 1982 bank nationalization in February 1982, according to his book *La nacionalización de la banca en México* (Mexico City: Siglo XXI, 1984).

20. Mexico, Secretaría de Industria y Comercio, *IX Censo de la población 1970* (Mexico City: División General de Estadística, 1970); Mexico, Comisión de Recursos Humanos del Gobierno Federal, *Censo de recursos humanos del sector público federal: administración central 1975* (Mexico City: Comisión de Recursos Humanos del Gobierno Federal, 1976); and, *Censo de recursos humanos del sector público federal: administración descentralizada y de participación estatal*

mayoritaria 1975 (Mexico City: Comisión de Recursos Humanos del Gobierno Federal, 1976).

21. A figure of 52.8 percent is derived from dividing the total number of professionals and *técnicos* in the 1970 census (734,674, or 5.65 percent of the workforce) into the number of such occupations reported in the 1975 census of public sector employees (387,593). The figure is perforce an estimate because of the timing difference, because respondents defined their own occupations, and because a large number of so-called *profesionistas* had completed fewer than five years of university study. See *IX Censo de la población 1970*, pp. 25–26.

22. See *Administración central 1975*, p. 67.

23. See *Administración decentralizada y de participación estatal mayoritaria 1975*, p. 165.

24. Smith, *Labyrinths of Power*, p. 88.

25. Adolfo Ruíz Cortines, 1952–1958, did not complete university studies.

26. Smith, *Labyrinths*, p. 119.

27. A chagrined lawyer commented: "The middle levels of Programming and Budgeting are filled with economists, but why? They are barely acting as economists and have been converted into accountants . . . . As for the accountants, the matter reduces to the same question. We know that they can add and subtract, but what do they know of legal measures?" (Interview No. 35)

28. For an imaginative treatment of this theme, see Larissa Lomnitz, "Horizontal and Vertical Relations and the Social Structure of Urban Mexico," *Latin American Research Review* 17:2 (1982), pp. 51–74.

29. The bibliography of writings on the Mexican military is thin. See Franklin D. Margiotta, *Civilian Control of the Military: Patterns in Mexico* (Buffalo: Council on International Studies, Special Studies No. 66, State University of New York, 1975); Jorge A. Lozano, *El ejército mexicano* (Mexico City: El Colegio de México, 1976); David F. Ronfeldt, "The Mexican Army and Political Order since 1940," in James W. Wilkie, et al., eds., *Contemporary Mexico* (Berkeley: University of California Press, 1976), pp. 317–336. This lack of studies on the Mexican military represents the most serious lacuna in the current literature on Mexican society.

30. Guillermo Villaseñor García analyzes the professions and the class system in "Una visión estructural de la institución profesional," *Revista del Centro de Estudios Educativos* 8:3 (1978), pp. 137–162.

31. These privileges may include short work hours, independent study, low-interest loans, subsidized consumer goods, generous pension benefits, and low-cost vacations.

Appendix:
Notes on the Interviews

Research for this book included private interviews with professional elites in each of the fields under study. The author compiled a list of prospective interviewees for each field, made contact with them by telephone, and requested an appointment to discuss their professions. The author identified his institutional affiliation and informed those interviewed that the research project was an academic endeavor independent of his work. In only one case was the appointment refused or not kept. The interviews covered the history of each profession, the role of university education, professional associations, prestige variables, political power and public policy, and the interviewee's recommendation of other persons with whom to speak. The informants were promised that their remarks, if quoted, would remain anonymous and that privileged information would not be attributed to them. A copy of each interview was delivered by hand with a letter of thanks. The interviewees reviewed the text and, in a few cases, reported minor corrections. The 46 formal interviews contributing to the research are listed below.

Number	Date	Length of interview (minutes)	Affiliation or occupation of interviewee
1	June 1978	45	Economist, public sector researcher
2	October 1978	120	Economist, academic institution, former government official

Number	Date	Length of interview (minutes)	Affiliation or occupation of interviewee
3	January 1981	15	Economist, academic institution
4	January 1981	80	Medical doctor, public sector researcher
5	January 1981	120	Economist, state-supported academic institution
6	January 1981	60	Economist, private academic institution
7	January 1981	60	Economist, state-supported academic institution
8	January 1981	60	Economist, public sector institution
9	January 1981	45	Economist, public sector institution (ex-Colegio president)
10	January 1981	60	Economist, public sector institution
11	January 1981	50	Medical doctor, academic institution
12	February 1981	65	Medical doctor, public sector researcher (ex-Academy president)
13	February 1981	55	Economist, academic institution
14	February 1981	75	Medical doctor, retired from private practice
15	February 1981	75	Medical doctor, academic institution
16	February 1981	85	Medical doctor, public institution and private practice (ex-Academy president)
17	February 1981	30	Agronomist, public sector policy position
18	February 1981	70	Agronomist, public sector institution
19	February 1981	55	Agronomist, academic institution
20	February 1981	105	Agronomist, academic institution

Number	Date	Length of interview (minutes)	Affiliation or occupation of interviewee
21	February 1981	50	Agronomist, public sector financial institution
22	February 1981	65	Agronomist, public sector research institution
23	February 1981	130	Agronomist, retired public sector official
24	March 1981	45	Agronomist, private sector bank
25	March 1981	30	Chemical engineer, public sector petroleum institution
26	March 1981	45	Agronomist, public sector policy position
27	March 1981	70	Petroleum engineer, public sector institution
28	March 1981	70	Petroleum engineer, academic institution
29	March 1981	45	Petroleum engineer, academic institution
30	March 1981	65	Petroleum engineer, retired public sector official
31	March 1981	65	Petroleum engineer, public sector and academic institution
32	March 1981	135	Petroleum engineer, public sector institution (ex-Association president)
33	March 1981	105	Petroleum engineer, retired public sector official
34	April 1981	40	Lawyer, academic institution
35	April 1981	75	Lawyer, public sector institution
36	April 1981	30	Lawyer, public sector institution
37	June 1981	60	Lawyer, academic institution
38	June 1981	30	Medical doctor, public institution and private practice (ex-Academy president)

Number	Date	Length of interview (minutes)	Affiliation or occupation of interviewee
39	April 1982	45	Architect, private practitioner and academic institution
40	April 1982	30	Civil engineer, public sector
41	April 1982	35	Civil engineer, public sector
42	April 1982	30	Architect, private practitioner and academic institution
43	May 1982	30	Civil engineer, public sector
44	June 1982	20	Petroleum engineer, public sector
45	June 1982	60	Lawyer, Dirección de Profesiones
46	June 1982	50	Civil engineer, public sector

Bibliography

BOOKS, MONOGRAPHS, THESES

Alanis Patiño, Emilio, et al. *Los agrónomos mexicanos: información histórica.* Mexico City: Ateneo Nacional Agronómico, 1954.

Alcagar, Mario Antonio. *Las agrupaciones patronales en México.* Mexico City: El Colegio de México, 1977.

Arriola, Carlos. *Los empresarios y el estado.* Mexico City: Fondo de Cultura Económica, 1981.

Barkin, David. *Desarrollo regional y reorganización campesina.* Mexico City: Nueva Imagen, 1978.

Baylis, Thomas A. *The Technical Intelligentsia and the East German Elite: Legitimacy and Social Change in Mature Communism.* Berkeley: University of California Press, 1974.

Benveniste, Guy. *Bureaucracy and National Planning: A Sociological Case Study in Mexico.* New York: Praeger, 1970.

Berger, Suzanne. *The French Political System.* New York: Random House, 1974.

Bermúdez, Antonio J. *The Mexican National Petroleum Industry: A Case Study in Nationalization.* Stanford: Institute of Hispanic American and Luso-Brazilian Studies, Stanford University, 1963.

Berthoud, Richard. *Unemployed Professionals and Executives.* London: Policy Studies Institute, No. 582, May 1979.

Blair, Roger D., and Stephen Rubin, eds. *Regulating the Professions: A Public Policy Symposium.* Lexington, Massachusetts: D.C. Heath and Company, 1980.

Blau, Peter M., and Otis Dudley Duncan, eds. *The American*

Occupational Structure. New York: John Wiley and Sons, 1967.

Boreham, Paul, Alex Pemberton, and Paul Wilson, eds. *The Professions in Australia: A Critical Appraisal.* St. Lucia, Queensland: University of Queensland Press, 1976.

Brothers, Dwight S., and Leopoldo Solís. *Mexican Financial Development.* Austin: University of Texas Press, 1966.

Camp, Roderic Ai. *Education and the State in Twentieth Century Mexico.* Unpublished manuscript, Central College, Pella, Iowa, 1983.

————. *The Role of the "Técnico" in Policy-making in Mexico: A Comparative Study of Developing Bureaucracy.* Doctoral Dissertation, University of Arizona, 1970.

————. *Mexico's Leaders: Their Education and Recruitment.* Tucson: The University of Arizona Press, 1980.

————. *La formación de un gobernante: la socialización de los líderes políticos en el México posrevolucionario.* Mexico City: Siglo XXI, 1981.

————. *Mexican Political Biographies 1935-1975.* Tucson: University of Arizona Press, 1976.

Cardoso, Fernando Henrique. *Autoritarismo e democratizaçao.* Rio de Janeiro: Editora Paz e Terra, 1975.

Carmona, Fernando, et al. *El milagro mexicano.* Mexico City: Editorial Nuestro Tiempo, 1970.

Carr-Saunders, Alexander Morris, and P.A. Wilson. *The Professions.* London: Oxford University Press, 1933.

Cerny, Philip G., and Martin A. Schain, eds. *French Politics and Public Policy.* New York: St. Martin's Press, 1980.

Chalmers, Douglas A., ed. *Changing Latin America: New Interpretations of its Politics and Society.* New York: Academy of Political Science, 1972.

Chávez, Ignacio. *México en la cultura médica.* Mexico City: El Colegio Nacional, 1947.

Churchwood, L.G. *The Soviet Intelligentsia: An Essay on the Social Structure and Roles of Soviet Intellectuals during the 1960s.* London: Rouledge and Kegan Paul, 1973.

Cleaves, Peter S. *Bureaucratic Politics and Administration in Chile.* Berkeley: University of California Press, 1974.

————, and Martin J. Scurrah. *Agriculture, Bureaucracy, and Military Government in Peru.* Ithaca, New York: Cornell University Press, 1980.

Collier, David, ed. *The New Authoritarianism in Latin America.* Princeton: Princeton University Press, 1979.

Collins, Randall. *The Credential Society: An Historical Sociology of Education and Stratification.* New York: Academic Press, 1979.

Córdova, Arnaldo. *La ideología de la revolución mexicano.* Mexico City: Editorial Era, 1973.

Cosío Villegas, Daniel. *El sistema político mexicano.* Mexico City: Joaquín Mortiz, 1976.

Derossi, Flavia. *El empresario mexicano.* Mexico City: Universidad National Autónoma de México, 1977.

DeWitt, Nicolas. *Education and Professional Employment in the U.S.S.R.* Washington, D.C.: Government Printing Office, 1961.

Dingwell, Robert, and Philip Lewis, eds. *The Sociology of the Professions: Lawyers, Doctors, and Others.* New York: St. Martin's Press, 1982.

Dubey, Satyamita M. *Social Mobility among the Professions: Study of the Professions in a Transitional Indian City.* Bombay: Popular Prakashan, 1975.

Elliott, Philip R.C. *The Sociology of the Professions.* London: Macmillan, 1972.

Esquivel Obregón, Toribio. *Apuntes para la historia del derecho en México.* Mexico City: Publicidad y Ediciones, 1943.

Fabrega, Jr., Horacio. *Disease and Social Behavior: An Interdisciplinary Perspective.* Cambridge: MIT Press, 1974.

Fernández y Fernández, Ramón. *Chapingo hace cincuenta años.* Chapingo: Colegio de Postgraduados, Escuela Nacional de Agricultura, 1976.

Flores de la Peña, Horacio. *Los obstáculos al desarrollo económico (el desequilibrio fundamental).* Doctoral dissertation, Escuela Nacional de Economía, Universidad Nacional Autónoma de México, 1955.

Freeman, Richard B. *The Over-Educated American.* New York: Academic Press, 1976.

Freidson, Eliot. *Professional Dominance: The Social Structure of Medical Care.* New York: Atherton Press, 1970.

———, ed. *The Professions and their Prospects.* Beverly Hills, California: Sage Publications, 1973.

———, and Judith Lorber, eds. *Medical Men and their Work.* Chicago: Aldine-Atherton, 1972.

Freyre Rubio, Javier. *Las organizaciones sindicales, obreras, y burocráticas contemporáneas en México.* Mexico City: Universidad Autónoma Metropolitana-Azcapotzalco, 1983.

Gilb, Corinne Lathrop. *Hidden Hierarchies: The Professions and Government.* New York: Harper and Row, 1966.

Glade, William P., and Charles W. Anderson. *The Political Economy of Mexico.* Madison: University of Wisconsin Press, 1963.

Godau, Rainer. *Estado y acero: historia política de las Truchas.* Mexico City: El Colegio de México, 1982.

Goldthorpe, John H., and Kenneth Hope. *The Social Grading of Occupations: A New Approach and Scale.* Oxford: Clarendon Press, 1974.

Gómez Tagle, Silvia. *Insurgencia y democracia en los sindicatos electricistas.* Mexico City: El Colegio de México, 1980.

González Casanova, Pablo, and Enrique Florescano, eds. *México Hoy.*
    Mexico City: Siglo XXI, 1979.
Goodman, David, and Michael Redclift. *From Peasant to Proletarian:*
    Capitalist Development and Agrarian Transitions. Oxford: Basil
    Blackwell, 1981.
Gouldner, Alvin W. *The Future of Intellectuals and the Rise of the New*
    Class. New York: Continuum, 1979.
Grayson, George W. *The Politics of Mexican Oil.* Pittsburgh: University
    of Pittsburgh Press, 1980.
Greenberg, Martin Harry. *Bureaucracy and Development: A Mexican*
    Case Study. Lexington, Massachusetts: D.C. Heath and Company,
    1970.
Grindle, Merilee S. *Bureaucrats, Politicians, and Peasants in Mexico.*
    Berkeley: University of California Press, 1977.
————, ed. *Politics and Policy Implementation in the Third World.*
    Princeton: Princeton University Press, 1980.
Gross, Ronald, and Paul Osterman, eds. *The New Professionals.* New
    York: Simon and Schuster, 1972.
Guitián, C.C. *Las porras: estudio de caso de un grupo de presión*
    universitario. Licenciate thesis, Escuela de Ciencias Sociales,
    Universidad Nacional Autónoma de México, 1975.
Gvishian, D.M., S.R. Mikulinsky, and S.A. Kugel. *The Scientific*
    Intelligentsia in the USSR (Structure and Dynamics of Personnel).
    Trans. Jane Sayers. Moscow: Progress Publishers, 1976.
Hall, Richard H. *Occupations and the Social Structure.* Englewood
    Cliffs, New Jersey: Prentice-Hall, 1969.
Hansen, Roger D. *The Politics of Mexican Development.* Baltimore:
    Johns Hopkins University Press, 1971.
Hargrove, Erwin C. *Professional Roles in Society and Government: The*
    English Case. Beverly Hills, California: Sage, 1972.
Heraud, Brian. *Sociology in the Professions.* London: Open Books,
    1979.
Hughes, Everett C., et al. *Education for the Professions of Medicine,*
    Law, Theology, and Social Welfare. New York: McGraw-Hill, 1973.
d'Hugues, Philippe, and Michel Peshier. *Les Professions en France:*
    evolution et perspectives. Paris: Presses Universitaires de France,
    1969.
Ilchman, Warren F., and Norman T. Uphoff. *The Political Economy of*
    Change. Berkeley: University of California Press, 1969.
Illich, Ivan. *Medical Nemesis: The Expropriation of Health.* New York:
    Pantheon Books, 1976.
————, et al. *The Disabling Professions.* London: Marion Boyers and
    Burns and MacEachern, 1977.
Iszaevich, Abraham. *Modernización campesina.* Mexico City: Editorial
    Edicol, 1980.
Jackson, J.A., ed. *Professions and Professionalization.* Cambridge:
    Cambridge University Press, 1970.

Jacob, Herbert. *German Administration since Bismarck: Central Authority versus Local Autonomy.* New Haven: Yale University Press, 1963.

Johnson, Terence J. *Professions and Power.* London: Macmillan, 1972.

———, and Marjorie Caygill. *Community in the Making: Aspects of Britain's Role in the Development of Professional Education in the Commonwealth.* London: University of London, Institute of Commonwealth Studies, 1972.

Kaufman, Martin. *Homeopathy in America: The Rise and Fall of a Medical Heresy.* Baltimore: Johns Hopkins University Press, 1971.

Kelly, Isabel T. *Folk Practices in North Mexico: Birth Customs, Folk Medicine, and Spiritualism in the Laguna Zone.* Austin: University of Texas Press, 1965.

Kett, Joseph. *The Formation of the American Medical Profession.* New Haven: Yale University Press, 1968.

Kleingartner, Archie. *Professionalism and Salaried Worker Organization.* Madison, Wisconsin: Industrial Relations Research Institute, 1967.

Konrad, Gyorgy, and Ivan Szelenyi. *The Intellectuals on the Road to Class Power.* Trans. Andrew Arato and Richard E. Allen. New York: Harcourt Brace Jovanovich, 1979.

Koslow, Lawrence, E., ed. *The Future of Mexico.* Tempe: Arizona State University, 1977.

Lajous Vargas, Adrián. *Aspectos de la educación superior y el empleo de profesionistas en México 1959-1967.* Licenciate thesis, Escuela Nacional de Economía, Universidad Nacional Autónoma de México, 1967.

Lambert, Nicolas. *The Technical Intelligentsia and the Soviet State: A Study of Soviet Managers and Technicians 1928-1935.* New York: Holmes and Meier, 1979.

Larson, Magali Sarfatti. *The Rise of Professionalism: A Sociological Analysis.* Berkeley: University of California Press, 1977.

Latapí, Pablo. *Análisis de un sexenio de la educación en México: 1970-1976.* Mexico City: Nueva Imagen, 1981.

LaVopa, Anthony J. *Prussian School Teachers: Profession and Office, 1763-1848.* Chapel Hill: University of North Carolina Press, 1980.

Levy, Daniel C. *University and Government in Mexico: Autonomy in an Authoritarian System.* New York: Praeger, 1980.

López Zamora, Emilio. *El agua, la tierra, los hombres de México.* Mexico City: Fondo de Cultura Económica, 1977.

Lozano, Jorge A. *El ejército mexicano.* Mexico City: El Colegio de México, 1976.

Mabry, Donald J. *The Mexican University and the State: Student Conflicts 1910-1971.* College Station: Texas A & M Press, 1981.

Maier, Joseph, and Richard W. Weatherhead, eds. *The Latin American University.* Albuquerque: University of New Mexico Press, 1979.

Malloy, James M., ed. *Authoritarianism and Corporatism in Latin America.* Pittsburgh: Pittsburgh University Press, 1977.

Margiotta, Franklin D. *Civilian Control of the Military: Patterns in Mexico.* Buffalo: Council on International Studies, Special Studies No. 66, State University of New York, 1975.

Mendoza Díaz, Alvaro. *La revolución de los profesionales e intelectuales en Latinoamérica.* Mexico City: Instituto de Investigaciones Sociales, Universidad Nacional Autónoma de México, 1962.

Meyer, Lorenzo. *Mexico and the United States in the Oil Controversy.* Trans. Muriel Vasconcelos. Austin: University of Texas Press, 1977.

————. *México y los Estados Unidos en el conflicto petrolero, 1917–1932.* Mexico City: El Colegio de México, 1968.

Meynard, Jean. *La Technocatie.* Paris: Payot, 1964.

Miller, Richard V. *The Role of Labor Organizations in a Developing Country: The Case of Mexico.* Doctoral Dissertation, Cornell University, 1964.

Millerson, Geoffrey. *The Qualifying Associations: A Study in Professionalization.* London: Routledge and Kegan Paul, 1964.

Moore, Wilbert E. *The Professions: Roles and Rules.* New York: Russell Sage Foundation, 1970.

Ocampo V., Tarsicio, ed. *México: socialización de la medicina 1965.* Cuernavaca: Centro Intercultural de Documentación CIDOC. Dossier No. 18, 1968.

O'Donnell, Guillermo. *Modernization and Bureaucratic Authoritarianism.* Berkeley: Institute of International Studies, University of California, 1973.

Orive Alba, Adolfo. *La irrigación en México.* Mexico City: Editorial Grijalva, 1970.

Pike, Fredrick B., and Thomas Stritch, eds. *The New Corporatism: Social-Political Structures in the Iberian World.* Notre Dame: University of Notre Dame Press, 1974.

Ramírez, Axel. *Bibliografía comentada de la medicina tradicional mexicana (1900–1978).* Mexico City: Instituto Mexicano para el Estudio de las Plantas Medicinales, 1978.

Reyna, José Luis, et al. *Tres estudios sobre el movimiento obrero en México.* Jornadas 80. Mexico City: El Colegio de México, 1976.

Reynolds, Clark W. *The Mexican Economy: Twentieth-Century Structure and Growth.* New Haven: Yale University Press, 1970.

Riding, Alan. *Distant Neighbors: A Portrait of the Mexicans.* New York: Alfred A. Knopf, 1985.

Rodríguez Sala de Gómezgil, María Luisa. *El científico en México: su imagen entre los estudiantes de enseñanza media.* Mexico City: Universidad Nacional Autónoma de México, 1977.

Rueschemeyer, Dietrich. *Lawyers and their Society: A Comparative Study of the Legal Profession in Germany and in the United States.* Cambridge: Harvard University Press, 1973.

Schendel, Gordon, et al. *Medicine in Mexico: From Aztec Herbs to Betatrons.* Austin: University of Texas Press, 1968.

Sepúlveda, Bernardo, ed. *Seminario sobre Educación Superior: Ponencias*. Mexico City: Colegio Nacional, 1979.

Silvert, Kalman H. *The Conflict Society: Reaction and Revolution in Latin America*. New Orleans: The Hauser Press, 1961.

Simpson, Eyler N. *The Ejido: Mexico's Way Out*. Chapel Hill: University of North Carolina Press, 1937.

Skilling, H. Gordon, and Franklyn Griffiths, eds. *Interest Groups in Soviet Politics*. Princeton: Princeton University Press, 1971.

Smith, Peter H. *Labyrinths of Power: Political Recruitment in Twentieth-Century Mexico*. Princeton: Princeton University Press, 1979.

Starr, Paul. *The Social Transformation of American Medicine*. New York: Basic Books, 1983.

Stepan, Alfred C. *The State and Society: Peru in Comparative Perspective*. Princeton: Princeton University Press, 1978.

Stevens, Evelyn P. *Protest and Response in Mexico*. Cambridge: MIT Press, 1974.

Stevens, Rosemary. *American Medicine and the Public Interest*. New Haven: Yale University Press, 1971.

Storey, Robert Gerald. *Professional Leadership*. Pasadena, California: Castle Press, 1958.

Suleiman, Ezra N. *Politics, Power, and Bureaucracy in France: The Administrative Elite*. Princeton: Princeton University Press, 1974.

Tecla Jiménez, Alfredo. *Universidad, burguesía y proletariado*. Mexico City: Cultura Popular, 1976.

Tello, Carlos. *La nacionalización de la banca en México*. Mexico City: Siglo XXI, 1984.

———. *La política económica en México 1970-1976*. Mexico City: Siglo XXI, 1979.

Treiman, Donald J. *Occupational Prestige in Comparative Perspective*. New York: Academic Press, 1977.

Véliz, Claudio. *The Centralist Tradition of Latin America*. Princeton: Princeton University Press, 1979.

Vernon, Raymond. *The Dilemma of Mexico's Development: The Roles of the Private and Public Sectors*. Cambridge: Harvard University Press, 1963.

———, ed. *Public Policy and Private Enterprise in Mexico*. Cambridge: Harvard University Press, 1964.

Viesca Treviño, Carlos, ed. *Estudios sobre la etnobotánica y antropología médica*. 3 vols. Mexico City: Centro de Estudios Económicos y Sociales del Tercer Mundo, 1976-1978.

Villarreal, René, ed. *Economía internacional II. Teorías del imperialismo, la dependencia y su evidencia histórica*. Mexico City: Fondo de Cultura Económica, 1979.

Vollmer, Howard M., and Donald L. Mills, eds. *Professionalization*. Englewood Cliffs, New Jersey: Prentice-Hall, 1966.

Wallerstein, Immanuel. *The Modern World System: Capitalist Agriculture and the Origins of the European World-Economy in the Sixteenth Century.* New York: Academic Press, 1974.

Warman, Arturo. *Y venimos a contradecir.* Mexico City: Ediciones Casa Chata, 1976.

Wilkie, James W., et al., eds. *Contemporary Mexico.* Berkeley: University of California Press, 1976.

Yates, P. Lamartine. *Mexico's Agricultural Dilemma.* Tucson: University of Arizona Press, 1981.

ARTICLES

Anderson, Bo, and James D. Cockroft. "Control and Co-optation in Mexican Politics," *International Journal of Comparative Sociology* 7 (March 1966), 11-28.

Atkinson, Paul, Margaret Reid, and Peter Sheldrake. "Medical Mystique," *Sociology of Work and Occupations* 4.3 (August 1977), 243-280.

Avendaño, José Luis, and Pablo A. Cabañas. "Bastiones de tiempo libre," *Nexos* 2:18 (June 1979), 13-23.

Bailey, John J. "Agrarian Reform in Mexico: The Quest for Self-Sufficiency," *Current History* 80:469 (November 1981), 357-360.

Barber, Bernard. "Some Problems in the Sociology of Professions," *Daedalus* 92:4 (Fall 1963), 669-688.

Barnes, L.W.C.S. "The Changing Stance of the Professional Employee," *Research Series* 29 (1975), Industrial Relations Centre, Queen's University at Kingston, 1-24.

Barr, Judith K., and Charles E. Barr. "The Structure of the Dental Profession and the Use of Auxiliaries in Latin America," *Social Science and Medicine* 14A:2 (March 1980), 107-111.

Bartra, Armando. "Colectivización o proletarización: el caso del Plan Chontalpa," *Cuadernos Agrarios* 1:4 (October-December 1976), 56-111.

Brooke, Nigel. "Actitudes de los empleadores mexicanos respecto a la educación: ¿un test de la teoría del capital humano?" *Revista del Centro de Estudios Educativos* 8:4 (1978), 109-132.

Cabrera, Lucio A. "History of the Mexican Judiciary," *Miami Law Quarterly* 439 (Summer 1957).

Camacho, Manuel. "Control sobre el movimiento obrero en México," *Foro Internacional* 16:4 (April–June, 1976), 496-525.

del Camino, Isidoro, and Jorge Muñoz B. "La enseñanza profesional en México en 1970," *Revista del Centro de Estudios Educativos* 2:3 (1972), 125-165.

Camp, Roderic Ai. "La educacion de la élite política mexicana," *Revista Mexicana de Sociología* 43:1 (January–March 1981), 421-454.

———. "An Image of Mexican Intellectuals: Some Preliminary Observations." *Journal of Mexican Studies* 1 (Winter 1985), 61-81.

———. "Mexican Presidential Pre-Candidates: Changes and Portent for the Future." *Polity* 16 (Summer 1984), 588-605.

———. "The Middle-Level Technocrat in Mexico," *Journal of Developing Areas* 6:4 (July 1972), 571-582.

———. "The National School of Economics and Public Life in Mexico," *Latin American Research Review* 10:3 (Fall 1975), 137-153.

———. "Political Recruitment and Change: Mexico in the 1970s." Unpublished manuscript, Central College, Pella, Iowa, 1982.

———. "El sistema mexicano y las decisiones sobre el personal político," *Foro Internacional* 17:1 (July–September 1976), 51-83.

———. "El técnico en México." *Revista Mexicana de Sociología* 45 (April–June 1983), 579-599.

———. "Women and Political Leadership in Mexico: A Comparative Study of Female and Male Political Elites," *Journal of Politics* 41:2 (May 1979), 417-441.

Cervera, Eduardo. "La enseñanza de la ingeniería petrolera en la Universidad Nacional Autónoma de México." Paper presented to the Panamerican Congress of Petroleum Engineering, Winter 1979.

Coatsworth, John. "Los orígenes del autoritarismo moderno en México," *Foro Internacional* 16 (October–December 1975), 205-232.

Cogan, Morris L. "Toward the Definition of a Profession," *Harvard Educational Review* 23 (Winter 1953), 33-50.

Cohen, Lenard J. "Partisans, Professionals, and Proletarians: Elite Change in Yugoslavia 1952-78," *Canadian Slavonic Papers* 21:4 (December 1979), 446-478.

Collier, David. "Industrial Modernization and Political Change: A Latin American Perspective," *World Politics* 30:4 (July 1978), 593-614.

———. "Timing of Economic Growth and Regime Characteristics in Latin America," *Comparative Politics* 7:3 (April 1975), 331-359.

Drysdale, Robert S. "The Legacy of Echeverría: What Mexico's President Inherited," *Worldview* (November 1977), 36-42.

Esteva, Gustavo. "¿Y si los campesinos existen?" *Comercio Exterior* 28:6 (June 1978), 699-732.

Fernández Lozano, María Teresa. "La formación de economistas en México," *El Economista Mexicano* 12:3 (May–June 1978), 21-26.

Field, Mark. "Taming a Profession: Early Phases of Soviet Socialized Medicine, *Bulletin of the New York Academy of Medicine* 48 (1972).

Fielding, A.G., and D. Portwood. "Professions and the State—Towards a Typology of Bureaucratic Professions," *Sociological Review* 28:1 (February 1980), 23-53.

Freidson, Eliot. "The Changing Nature of Professional Control." *Annual Review of Sociology* 10 (1984).

Frankenberg, Ronald. "Allopathic Medicine, Profession, and Capitalist Ideology in India," *Social Science and Medicine* 15A:2 (1981), 115-125.

Garfield, Richard. "Nursing, Health Care and Professionalism in Cuba," *Social Sciences and Medicine* 15A:1 (January 1981), 63-72.

Godau, Rainer, and Viviane B. de Márquez. "Estado mexicano y desarrollo industrial." Unpublished manuscript, El Colegio de México, October 1979.

Gómez, Victor Manuel. "Educación superior, mercado de trabajo y práctica profesional: análisis comparativo de diversos estudios en México." Unpublished paper, Centro de Estudios Sociales y Económicos del Tercer Mundo, August 1982.

Grindle, Merilee S. "Power, Expertise and the 'Técnico': Suggestions from a Mexican Case Study," *Journal of Politics* 39:2 (May 1977), 399-426.

Gurrieri, Adolfo. "El progreso técnico y sus frutos: la idea de desarrollo en la obra de Raúl Prebisch," *Comercio Exterior* 31:212 (December 1981), 1350-1356.

Gyarmati K., Gabriel. "The Doctrine of the Professions: Basis of a Power Structure," *International Social Science Journal* 27:4 (1975), 630-654.

Handelman, Howard. "Organized Labor in Mexico: Oligarchy and Dissent," *American Universities Field Staff Reports* 18 (1979).

Hernández Laos, Enrique, and Jorge Córdova Chávez. "Estructuras de la distribución del ingreso en México," *Comercio Exterior* 29:5 (May 1979), 505-520.

Honey V., Eduardo. "Los procesos sociales mexicanos y su relación con los servicios profesionales." Unpublished manuscript, Prospectiva Universitaria, Mexico City, 1978.

Jamous, H., and B. Pelaille. "Professions or Self-Perpetuating System? Changes in the French University-Hospital System," in J.A. Jackson, ed., *Professions and Professionalization*, (Cambridge: Cambridge University Press, 1970), 109-152.

Johnson, Terence C. "What Is To Be Known? The Structural Determination of Social Class," *Economy and Society* 6:2 (May 1977), 194-233.

Kelly, Guillermo. "Politics and Administration in Mexico: Recruitment and Promotion of the Politico-Administrative Class." Institute of Latin American Studies, University of Texas at Austin, *Technical Paper Series* 33 (1981), 1-16.

Klegon, Douglas. "The Sociology of Professions: An Emerging Perspective." *Sociology of Work and Occupations* 5:3 (August 1978), 259-283.

Kuisel, R.F. "Technocrats and Public Economic Policy: From the Third to the Fourth Republic," *Journal of European Economic History* 2:1 (Spring 1973).

Labastida Martín del Campo, Julio. "La crisis y la tregua (México 1976-1977), I" *Nexos* 2:21 (September 1979), 3-9.

————. "Proceso político y dependencia en México, 1970-1976," *Revista Mexicana de Sociología,* 39:1 (January–March 1977).

Latapí, Pablo. "Profesiones y sociedad." Unpublished manuscript, Prospectiva Universitaria, 1982.

Lomnitz, Larissa. "Conflict and Mediation in a Latin American University," *Journal of Inter-American Studies and World Affairs* 19:3 (August 1977), 315-338.

————. "The Exercise of Power in a Latin American University." Paper prepared for the Burg Wartenstein Symposium No. 84, Werner Gren Foundation, New York, July 1980.

————. "Horizontal and Vertical Relations and the Social Structure of Urban Mexico," *Latin American Research Review* 17:2 (1982), 51-74.

Márquez, Viviane. "Estructura del sector público de la salud en México: problemas y perspectivas." Paper presented at the Fifth Congress of Social Work, Mexico City, April 2 to 4, 1981.

Middlebrook, Kevin. "State Structure and Labor Participation in Mexico." Paper presented at the 7th meeting of the Latin American Studies Association, Houston, Texas, November 2-5, 1977.

Murphy, Terence D. "The French Medical Profession's Perception of its Social Function between 1776 and 1830," *Medical History* 23:3 (July 1979), 259-278.

Needleman, Carolyn, and Martin Needleman. "Who Rules Mexico? A Critique of some Current Views on the Mexican Political Process," *Journal of Politics* 31:4 (November 1969), 1011-1034.

O'Donnell, Guillermo A. "Corporatism and the Question of the State," in James Malloy, ed. *Authoritarianism and Corporatism in Latin America* (Pittsburgh: University of Pittsburgh Press, 1977); 47-89.

Oszlak, Oscar. "Notas críticas para una teoría de la burocracia estatal," *Revista Mexicana de Sociología* 60:30 (July–September 1978), 881-926.

Oyebola, D.D.O. "Professional Association, Ethics and Discipline among Yoruba Traditional Healers of Nigeria," *Social Sciences and Medicine* 15B:2 (April 1981), 87-92.

Parsons, Talcott. "Professions," in David L. Sills, ed. *International Encyclopedia of the Social Sciences* (New York: Crowell Collier and Macmillan, 1968), 536-547.

Pérez Correa, Fernando. "La universidad: contradicciones y perspectivas," *Foro Internacional 55* 14:3 (January–March 1974), 375-401.

Purcell, Susan Kaufman, and John F.H. Purcell. "State and Society in Mexico: Must a Stable Polity be Institutionalized?", *World Politics* 32:2 (January 1980), 194-227.

Redclift, Michael R. "El estado frente al campo," *Nexos* 47 (November 1981), 11-16.

Reynaga Obregón, Sonia, and Jesús Suaste Aguirre. "Educación superior y empleo." Unpublished paper presented to the Foro sobre Educación y Sociedad, Jalapa, Mexico, May 7 to 9, 1981.

Reynolds, Clark W. "Why Mexico's 'Stabilizing Development' was Actually Destablizing (with some Implications for the Future)," Council on Foreign Relations, Current Issues Review Group on U.S.-Mexican Relations, April 5, 1977.

Ridley, F.F. "French Technocracy and Comparative Government," *Political Studies* 14 (February 1966).

Rodríguez Forero, Jaime. "El concepto de masificación: su importancia y perspectivas para el análisis de la educación superior," *Fichas* Buenos Aires: UNESCO, CEPAL, PNUD, 1978.

Rosenblüeth, Ingrid. "Dependencia tecnológica e involución profesional: la industria y la ingeniería química en México," *Relaciones: Estudios de Historia y Sociedad* I:1 (Winter 1980), 35-90.

Roxborough, Ian, and Francisco Zapata. "Algunas notas sobre el sindicalismo en México," *Diálogos* 84 (November–December 1978).

Rueschemeyer, Dietrich. "Doctors and Lawyers: A Comment on the Theory of the Professions," *The Canadian Review of Sociology and Anthropology* 1:1 (February 1964), 17-30.

Sanders, Thomas G. "Population Growth and Resource Management: Planning Mexico's Water Supply," *American Universities Field Staff Reports*, North American Series 2:3 (1974), 1-16.

Schmitter, Philippe C. "Paths to Political Development in Latin America," in Douglas A. Chalmers, ed., *Changing Latin America: New Interpretations of its Politics and Society*. New York: Academy of Political Science, 1972, 83-109.

———. "Still the Century of Corporatism?" in Fredrick B. Pike and Thomas Stritch, eds., *The New Corporatism: Social-Political Structures in the Iberian World* (Notre Dame: University of Notre Dame Press, 1974); 85-131.

Simoni, Joseph, and Richard A. Ball. "The Mexican Medical Huckster: He Must Be Doing Something Right," *Sociology of Work and Occupations* 4:3 (August 1977), 343-365.

Vice Acosta, Cynthia. "CONACYT: 26,000 Study Grants," *R&D Mexico* 2:1 (October 1981), 47-48.

Villaseñor García, Guillermo. "Una visión estructural de la institución profesional," *Revista del Centro de Estudios Educativos* 8:3 (1978), 137-162.

Wiarda, Howard J. "Toward a Framework for the Study of Political Change in the Iberic-Latin Tradition: The Corporative Model," *World Politics* 25:2 (January 1973), 206-235.

Wilensky, Harold L. "The Professionalization of Everyone?" *The American Journal of Sociology* 70:2 (September 1964), 137-158.

Wilkerson, S. Jeffrey K. "Occupational Prestige in Mexico as Perceived by College Students." *Human Mosaic* 2 (Fall 1967), 56-64.

Wionczek, Miguel S. "La aportación de la política hidráulica entre 1925 y 1970 a la actual crisis agrícola mexicana," *Comercio Exterior* 32:4 (April 1982), 394-409.

DOCUMENTS

ANUIES. *Anuario estadístico 1980*. Mexico City: Asociación Nacional de Universidades e Institutos de Enseñanza Superior, 1981.
————. *La enseñanza superior en México 1970-1976*. Mexico City: Secretaría General Ejecutiva, 1976.
Asociación Mexicana de Educación Agrícola Superior. *Información General*. Mexico City: AMEAS, 1980.
Escuela Nacional de Agricultura. *Información estadística de la población escolar: período 1966 a 1976*. Chapingo: Departamento de Planeación, 1976.
Mexico, Comisión de Recursos Humanos del Gobierno Federal. *Censo de recursos humanos del sector público federal: administración central 1975*. Mexico City: Comisión de Recursos Humanos del Gobierno Federal, 1976.
————, ————. *Censo de recursos humanos del sector público federal: administración decentralizada y de participación estatal mayoritaria 1975*. Mexico City: Comisión de Recursos Humanos del Gobierno Federal, 1976.
————, CONACYT. *La ciencia y la tecnología en el sector medicina y salud: diagnóstico y política*. Mexico City: Consejo Nacional de Ciencia y Tecnología, 1976.
————, Secretaría de Educación Pública. *Ley de profesiones (reformas)*. Mexico City: Dirección General de Información, 1974.
————, Secretaría de Industria y Comercio. *Anuario Estadístico 1975-1976*. Mexico City: Dirección General de Estadística, 1977.
————, ————. *IX Censo general de población 1970*. Mexico City: División General de Estadística, 1970.
————, Secretaría del Patrimonio Nacional. *Memoria de Labores: 1 Setiembre de 1975 – 30 agosto de 1976*. Mexico City: Dirección General de Difusión, 1976.
————, Secretaría de Programación y Presupuesto. *La industria petrolera en México*. Mexico City: Coordinación General del Sistema Nacional de Información, 1979.
————, ————. *El papel del sector público en la economía mexicana (versión preliminar)*. Mexico City: Coordinación General del Sistema Nacional de Información, April 1979, volumes 1 and 2.
Quebec Province. *The Evolution of Professionalism in Quebec*. Quebec City: Office des Professions, 1976.
Unión de Universidades de América Latina. *Censo Universitario Latinoamericano 1966-1969*. Mexico City: UDUAL, 1971.

United Nations. *Statistical Yearbook*. New York: United Nations, 1972-1982.

Universidad Autónoma de Nuevo León. *Universidad en cifras*. Monterrey: Dirección de Planeación Universitaria, 1980-1981.

Universidad Nacional Autónoma de México. *Anuario Estadístico 1970-1980*. Mexico City: Secretario General de Servicios Auxiliares, 1971-1981.

Weil, Thomas E., et al. *Area Handbook for Mexico*. Washington: U.S. Government Printing Office, 1975.

Index

Academy of Medicine, *See* National Academy of Medicine
Accountancy, 67, 124 n.18
Agrarian reform, 25–27
Agraz, Juan Salvador, 22
Agriculture, 16, 27, 32, 40
Agronomy, profession of, 40, 63, 69–72, 82, 87–88, 90, 98; and nationalism, 21, 25–28. *See also* University training
Aguirre Velázquez, Ramón, 67
Alejo, Javier, 33
Alemán presidency, 68, 74
Alvarez Luna, Eduardo, 71
Architecture, profession of, 4, 62, 116 n.16
Armed forces. *See* Military
Arteaga, Jaime, 71
Australia, 110 n.17
Avila Camacho presidency, 91
Ayala González, Abraham, 36

Bank of Mexico, 29, 30, 53, 54, 95
Banking system, 33, 90
Bassols, Narciso, 30, 116 n.36
Beteta, Ramón, 30
Bidding procedures, 24–25, 87, 89
Bonifaz Nuño, Rubén, 20
Borlaug, Norman, 27
Brazil, 12
Bureaucracy, 12, 40
Bustamante, Eduardo, 30

Calles presidency, 26, 87
Camarilla, 17, 49, 61, 67–70, 82, 94, 121 n.18
Campesinistas, 28, 40, 71
Campos Salas, Octaviano, 30
CANACINTRA, xii, 29, 89
Cárdenas presidency, 21, 25, 28, 29, 91
Cardoso, Fernando Henrique, 34
Carrillo Flores, Antonio, 30
Centralism, 11, 12, 60
Certification, 6, 7, 46, 54–55, 58–59
Chambismo, 74–75, 116 n.32
Chapingo. *See* National School of Agriculture
Chávez, Ignacio, 36
Chile, 100
Church, 3, 4, 7, 108
CIMMYT, xii, 28
Class mobility, 7, 43–45, 99, 101
Colegio de Mexico, 53
College of Agronomic Engineers, 64, 71
College of Petroleum Engineers, 64–65
CONACYT, xiii, 53
Constitution. *See* 1917 Constitution
Corporatism, 12, 60
Corruption, 78, 98, 99
Cosío Villegas, Daniel, 20, 30
Cuba, 10, 34

De la Garza, Jesús, 23
De la Madrid presidency, 33, 67, 81, 90, 91–93

About the Author

PETER S. CLEAVES has lived for more than twenty years outside the United States as a student, foundation official, and banker. After attending Dartmouth College, he received the M.A. from Vanderbilt University and the Ph.D. in political science from the University of California, Berkeley. He is the author of three books and numerous articles on Latin American affairs. His professional career encompasses a decade of association with the Ford Foundation and an active role in domestic and international business.